Asset Allocation with
Private Equity

Other titles in Foundations and Trends® in Finance

Institutional Investors and Corporate Governance
Amil Dasgupta, Vyacheslav Fos and Zacharias Sautner
ISBN: 978-1-68083-878-7

The Implications of Heterogeneity and Inequality for Asset Pricing
Stavros Panageas
ISBN: 978-1-68083-750-6

Risk Sharing Within the Firm: A Primer
Marco Pagano
ISBN: 978-1-68083-740-7

The Economics of Credit Rating Agencies
Francesco Sangiorgi and Chester Spatt
ISBN: 978-1-68083-380-5

Initial Public Offerings: A Synthesis of the Literature and Directions for Future Research
Michelle Lowry, Roni Michaely and Ekaterina Volkova
ISBN: 978-1-68083-340-9

Privatization, State Capitalism, and State Ownership of Business in the 21st Century
William L. Megginson
ISBN: 978-1-68083-338-6

Asset Allocation with Private Equity

Arthur Korteweg
University of Southern California
korteweg@marshall.usc.edu

Mark M. Westerfield
University of Washington
mwesterf@uw.edu

the essence of knowledge

Boston — Delft

Foundations and Trends® in Finance

Published, sold and distributed by:
now Publishers Inc.
PO Box 1024
Hanover, MA 02339
United States
Tel. +1-781-985-4510
www.nowpublishers.com
sales@nowpublishers.com

Outside North America:
now Publishers Inc.
PO Box 179
2600 AD Delft
The Netherlands
Tel. +31-6-51115274

The preferred citation for this publication is

A. Korteweg and M. M. Westerfield. *Asset Allocation with Private Equity*. Foundations and Trends® in Finance, vol. 13, no. 2, pp. 95–204, 2022.

ISBN: 978-1-68083-968-5
© 2022 A. Korteweg and M. M. Westerfield

Foundations and Trends® in Finance
Volume 13, Issue 2, 2022
Editorial Board

Editorial Scope

Topics

Foundations and Trends® in Finance publishes survey and tutorial articles in the following topics:

- Corporate Finance
  - Corporate Governance
  - Corporate Financing
  - Dividend Policy and Capital Structure
  - Corporate Control
  - Investment Policy
  - Agency Theory and Information

- Asset Pricing
  - Asset-Pricing Theory
  - Asset-Pricing Models
  - Tax Effects
  - Liquidity
  - Equity Risk Premium
  - Pricing Models and Volatility
  - Fixed Income Securities

- Financial Markets
  - Market Microstructure
  - Portfolio Theory
  - Financial Intermediation
  - Investment Banking
  - Market Efficiency
  - Security Issuance
  - Anomalies and Behavioral Finance

- Derivatives
  - Computational Finance
  - Futures Markets and Hedging
  - Financial Engineering
  - Interest Rate Derivatives
  - Credit Derivatives
  - Financial Econometrics
  - Estimating Volatilities and Correlations

Information for Librarians

Foundations and Trends® in Finance, 2022, Volume 13, 4 issues. ISSN paper version 1567-2395. ISSN online version 1567-2409. Also available as a combined paper and online subscription.

Contents

Asset Allocation with Private Equity

Arthur Korteweg[1] and Mark M. Westerfield[2]

[1] University of Southern California, USA; korteweg@marshall.usc.edu
[2] University of Washington, USA; mwesterf@uw.edu

ABSTRACT

We survey the literature on the private equity partnership arrangement from the perspective of an outside investor (limited partner). We examine how the partnership arrangement fits into a broader portfolio of investments, and we consider the methods and difficulties in performance measurement, both at the fund level and at the asset class level. We follow with a discussion of performance persistence and the skill and pricing power of both general and limited partners. We continue by examining the limited partner's problem of managing commitments and investments over time while diversifying across funds in light of both idiosyncratic and systematic shocks. We close with a summary of recent work on optimal portfolio allocation to private equity. Throughout, we consider how empirical and theoretical work match the particular institutional details of private equity, and we identify 27 open questions to help guide private equity research forward.

Arthur Korteweg and Mark M. Westerfield (2022), "Asset Allocation with Private Equity", Foundations and Trends® in Finance: Vol. 13, No. 2, pp 95–204. DOI: 10.1561/0500000062.

1

Introduction

Institutional investors allocate an increasingly large share of their portfolios to private equity (PE) investments, such as venture capital (VC) and leveraged buyouts (BO).[1] In the decade following the global financial crisis of 2008, pension funds and endowments nearly doubled their allocations to private equity and real estate. These allocations represented almost 20% of assets under management for pension funds in many large, developed economies in 2017 and a similar fraction for endowments of U.S. higher education institutions in 2019.[2] Another sign of the increasingly important role of PE in portfolios is the current debate in the U.S. over whether to allow defined contribution pension plans, such as 401(k) plans, to invest in PE. At the same time, many companies have chosen to stay, or convert to, private firms, resulting in a decline in the number of publicly listed firms (e.g., Kahle and Stulz,

---

[1]For the purpose of this monograph, when we say private equity, we include all types, including venture capital, buyout, real estate, private debt, infrastructure, natural resources, and others.

[2]See Ivashina and Lerner (2018) for pension funds. The endowment number refers to the value-weighted average allocation across endowments, per the 2019 NACUBO-TIAA Study of Endowments, http://products.nacubo.org/index.php/leadership/2019-nacubo-tiaa-study-of-endowments.html.

2017). The combined result of these trends is that a large share of the economy is not traded in public markets.

The purpose of this monograph is to address the central question "What is the optimal portfolio allocation to private equity?" In doing so, we have two goals. The first is to survey the literature on the private equity partnership arrangement from an investor's perspective, including how these partnerships fit into a broader portfolio. The second is to articulate a list of open questions in the literature. We identify 27 open questions that we believe will help to push research in private equity forward.

Investing in private equity means taking a stake as a Limited Parter (LP) in a fund or other vehicle run by a General Partner (GP). These stakes are delegated investments governed by Limited Partnership Agreements (LPAs) that specify contractual arrangements, including decision-making powers and fees. There are three core features of private equity investments that distinguish them from other investments an LP might make:

(1) The LP makes capital commitments, and the GP has discretion over when to call capital from the LP and when to distribute it. Thus, it is the intermediary (GP), not the source of capital (LP), that determines the timing of investment and the quantity invested at any particular time.

(2) LP stakes are not easily or frequently traded with other LPs, despite a growing secondary market, and LPs cannot redeem capital from funds prematurely. Thus, there is no well defined market price to determine fund-level performance and no easy exit mechanism for LPs.

(3) Private equity funds are all differently created, bespoke investment vehicles, and investments in main PE funds are frequently paired with co-investment or other alternative vehicles. Similarly, there is significant variation in the level and structure of fees. Thus, comparing LPs' investments and opportunities is difficult.

Some assets share some of these difficulties – parts of real estate and some illiquid bonds, for example – but the combination of the three makes private equity particularly interesting and worth studying.

The three core features interact with each other. For example, the GP's investment discretion (1), combined with the unavailability of market prices (2), gives the GP the scope to manipulate performance measures. As a result, it is difficult to determine how much risk a GP is taking and what is their skill level. The GP's investment discretion (1), combined with the bespoke nature of funds and co-investment vehicles (3), gives the GP the ability to offer slightly different investment packages to different LPs. As a result, there is scope for both GPs and LPs to exert bargaining or pricing power. The lack of mark-to-market valuations (2), combined with the fact that private equity funds are all risky and differentiated (3), implies that investment managers (LPs, such as pension funds and endowments) can take risks that are hidden from their principals.

As will become clear, there is no simple, cookie-cutter answer to the portfolio decision question. All LPs are not created equal, and depending on factors such as size, access, and skill, the optimal portfolio weight can be zero or it can be substantial. In light of this, questions of particular interest are:

(1) How does the LP assess performance data given the measurement and agency problems created by delegating investment decisions to the GP? For example, how does one assess a GP's skill when the timing of all capital calls and distributions are at the GP's discretion?

(2) How should the LP understand the bargaining problem with GPs? What gives a GP or LP pricing power, and how can that be exploited?

(3) How much of a premium do and should LPs require for their grant of liquidity and investment discretion to the GP? How much of a premium is required to accept the inevitable performance manipulation?

We have organized our monograph to lead from a description of theoretical and empirical work toward open questions. To that end, we have included a substantial number of recent and unpublished working papers in our survey.[3] Perhaps paradoxically, research in private equity is simultaneously incomplete and of great relevance to wider questions regarding the incentives, financing, and pricing of investments.

The monograph proceeds as follows: Section 2 contains institutional details regarding PE firms, funds, and investors. For some readers this will be a review, but we include it because the institutional details are required to understand the decision rights that the LP grants the GP and how those decisions are usually executed. We also set up a discussion of the GP's incentives which will pervade our discussion of selected data and pricing power later in the monograph.

To understand why the institutional details of PE matter for LPs, one has to understand the uses and limitations of the benchmark portfolio choice model. To this end, Section 3 reviews a standard portfolio choice model, and we show how the characteristics of PE violate the model's core assumptions.

Section 4 describes the methods and problems with measuring performance in PE. We begin with industry-level performance, describing the methods and problems in constructing a private equity index, and discuss results on the risk loadings of aggregate PE investments. We then move on to the fund level, introducing common performance measures and recent innovations. We show how performance measures fail and how they can be manipulated, both by misreporting and by changing underlying economic activity. We conclude with a discussion of GP skill and fund return persistence.

Section 5 shifts the focus from PE investments to PE investors, and we examine the returns and pricing power of LPs. A core piece of the asset allocation problem for an LP is how to choose and manage relationships with individual GPs. We begin with an examination of persistent return differences for LPs and how they have changed over time. We then discuss theories and empirical results covering LP pricing

---

[3]We describe the results of unpublished papers as they appear at the time of this writing, with the caveat that some of these will change significantly between their current version and their published version.

power and differential access, including liquidity, information, search, and size. We conclude with an evaluation of the different goals of various LPs, particularly the non-financial goals of public institutions.

Section 6 focuses on LPs' diversification problem and their liquidity management problem, including the role of the secondary market. How should private equity commitments be spread across funds and through time? Diversification and liquidity are strongly connected because of the particular nature of cash flow and liquidity shocks in PE. We explore the implied trade-offs at the fund level and the relationship between the fund level and aggregate activity. We examine the various types of liquidity that have been introduced in the wider finance literature and how they apply to PE. We close with a summary of some recent work on optimal portfolio allocation to PE.

2

Private Equity Institutional Details

This section provides an overview of the features of the private equity industry that are relevant to understanding an investor's portfolio decision problem. We describe the PE fund structure, fees paid to the fund managers and the incentives they engender, and other opportunities to gain PE exposure through co-investments, solo investments, alternative vehicles, and publicly traded funds.

2.1 Fund Partnerships

Private equity firms generally structure their investments in funds. PE funds are set up as Limited Partnerships with approximately a 10-year life. The partners of the PE firm serve as the General Partners (GPs) of the fund. They are responsible for deal sourcing and they make all the investment and liquidation decisions.

The outside investors are Limited Partners (LPs) in the fund. GPs usually impose a fairly high minimum investment on the order of $5 million,[1] so typical LPs are large (mostly institutional) investors such as pension funds, endowments, insurance companies, high net worth

---

[1]See, for example, DeLuce (2020) and Preqin (2016). Minimum investment requirements increase in the size of the GP's fund.

individuals, and sovereign wealth funds. They are pure capital providers and are not involved in the investment decision-making process or in any of the other decisions with respect to the fund's portfolio. Instead, LPs enter into a contract with GPs (the Limited Partnership Agreement or LPA) during fundraising, and this agreement spells out all parties' rights and responsibilities. GPs also invest in the fund – partly to align incentives with LPs – but their commitment is usually very small as a percentage of the fund's size. A typical GP stake in North America is 1% of the fund (Robinson and Sensoy, 2013), but it can be substantially higher.[2]

LPs do not immediately hand over their committed capital to the GP when the fund is initiated. Instead, the GP calls the capital from LPs, pro rata to their commitment, when investments are made. For example, suppose an LP made a $10 million commitment to a $100 million fund, and the GP makes a $1 million investment. The LP will be expected to wire $100,000 to the GP, 1% of its commitment. The first few years of a fund's life, known as the "investment period", are dominated by capital calls as the GP builds up the investment portfolio.

Capital calls arrive stochastically, and LPs need to plan to have sufficient liquidity to meet these calls. Penalties for defaulting on a capital call are steep (see, for example, Banal-Estañol *et al.*, 2017 and Litvak, 2004), and may include interest charges, withholding of future distributions, reducing or forfeiting the LP's capital commitment, forcing a sale of the LP's stake to a third party, eliminating voting rights, and removing the LP from the LP advisory committee. There may also be reputational harm to the LP that may prevent them from investing with desired GPs in the future.

The assets of the fund vary across the PE class. In the case of venture capital (VC), the fund buys a (minority) equity share in start-up companies. In buyout (BO), investments are levered equity stakes (often full ownership) in larger, more mature firms that have been operating for years, if not decades. Firms that receive PE investment from either VC or BO are referred to as "portfolio firms" or "portfolio companies". GPs are actively involved with the fund's portfolio companies and properties.

---

[2] Jia and Wang (2017) find an average GP stake of 6.6% for a sample of Chinese venture capital (VC) funds, although these are for the most part not directly comparable to their U.S. counterparts in terms of their size and structure.

For example, in VC, they serve on the board of the invested start-ups and help them grow by providing strategic advice, assisting in hiring, and other value-added services. In buyout, they may replace an under-performing company's management and divest non-core assets. Other popular asset classes are real estate (primarily commercial real estate), private debt, natural resources, and infrastructure. Finally, there are secondary funds, which buy LP stakes in already-active funds on the secondary market, and fund-of-funds (FoFs), which commit capital to a portfolio of other newly raised PE funds.

Ultimately, the fund makes money when it sells its shares in a portfolio company. Such exits are accomplished either through an initial public offering (IPO, sometimes called a "reverse buyout" in buyout) or a sale of the firm (or the property in real estate funds). Cash from the sale of stock is usually passed through to LPs net of GP fees, although the LPA may allow the GP to reinvest early distributions in new deals. Since there is randomness in the timing of exits, distributions are stochastic, with the bulk arriving in the later years of a fund's life.

Figure 2.1 shows the evolution of the number of U.S. based funds (Panel A) and aggregated committed capital (Panel B) for each PE class, by vintage year (that is, the year of fund initiation). Growth exploded after the 1978 Revenue Act reduced the capital gains rate from 49.5% to 28%, and the 1979 ERISA "prudent man" rule opened the door for pension funds to invest in VC. The mid-to-late 1980s saw a wave of leveraged buyout investments. This initial growth period continued until the internet bust in 2000. After retrenchment ended in 2002, growth returned to the PE industry. This early 2000s growth period lasted up until the global financial crisis of 2008, and was especially strong in buyout, real estate, and private debt funds. Infrastructure funds also arrived on the scene during this time. Since the end of the financial crisis, there has been a strong rebound in buyout, real estate, and private debt funds, in particular. Figure 2.1 also shows that while VC, buyout, and real estate have been the most popular PE flavors historically, private debt has grown more prominent since the mid-2000s, while infrastructure and natural resources funds are less common.

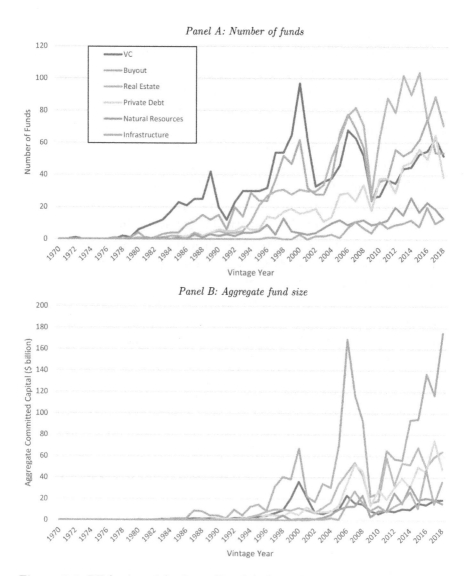

Figure 2.1: PE funds and fund size. Panel A shows the time series of the number of funds raised in vintage years from 1970 to 2018, and Panel B shows the aggregate amount of capital committed to those funds. Funds of funds, secondary funds, co-investments, and venture debt funds are excluded.

Source: Preqin.

Table 2.1: Descriptive statistics of PE funds. The table reports descriptive statistics for a sample of closed private equity funds with a North American geographic focus for vintages from 1969 to 2019, by PE asset class. Funds of funds, secondary funds, co-investments, and venture debt funds are excluded. Reported fund sizes and returns are averages, with medians in parentheses, in millions of U.S. dollars. TVPI is the total value to paid-in capital multiple, IRR is the internal rate of return, and PME is the Kaplan and Schoar (2005) public market equivalent using the S&P 500 as the benchmark

	VC	Buyout	Real Estate	Private Debt	Natural Resources	Infra- structure
Number of funds	1,475	1,302	1,435	723	291	144
Fund size ($m)	247	1,331	574	868	914	2,067
	(150)	(500)	(269)	(438)	(410)	(999)
Liquidated (%)	46	38	38	29	33	13
Number of GPs	569	431	380	244	92	65
Fund returns:						
TVPI	1.89	1.81	1.42	1.41	1.54	1.28
	(1.38)	(1.61)	(1.38)	(1.30)	(1.30)	(1.22)
IRR (%)	14.85	16.21	11.79	11.19	14.94	9.59
	(9.27)	(14.00)	(11.58)	(10.02)	(9.54)	(8.78)
PME	0.96	1.11	0.96	1.01	0.94	0.86
	(0.98)	(1.10)	(0.97)	(0.98)	(0.86)	(0.90)

Source: Preqin.

Table 2.1 provides summary statistics of funds by asset class, for all vintages until 2019. VC funds tend to be the smallest, at an average (median) fund size of $247 million ($150 million). VCs invest relatively small amounts, usually less than $2 million at the early stages of a start-up's life, although this amount can grow into the tens of millions or even larger for some companies in later stages. A fund's investments in an individual buyout deal tends to be considerably larger, and, as a consequence, buyout funds are larger, at an average (median) size of $1.3 billion ($500 million). The largest funds are in infrastructure, where the average (median) fund is $2.1 billion ($999 million).

2.2   Fees

GPs charge a variety of fees, and, in this section, we describe the most common components of private equity fee structures. As emphasized in Phalippou (2009) and Litvak (2009), fee structures vary across funds and are often opaque. What may appear like small changes in definitions and timing can have large impacts on the present value of fees. In addition, as we will see in Section 5.1, there is even variation in the fees paid by different LPs in the same fund.

2.2.1   Calculating Fees

Management fees are typically 2% per year, with some variation around this number. This percentage is initially computed based on committed capital. Many funds lower the basis or the fee percentage or both after the investment period ends. The investment period is usually defined as the first four or five years of the fund's life (three years for real estate funds and private debt). The rationale for lower fees after this period is that most of the GP's effort is expended during the investment period, in terms of deal sourcing, due diligence, and other deal-related activities.[3] A common schedule is to start out with committed capital as the basis and switch it to net invested capital after the investment period ends. An important feature to note is that the management fee is taken out of the capital commitment, and fees are one type of capital call. For example, a $100 million fund with a 2% annual management fee on committed capital charges $20 million in fees over its 10-year life and invests the remaining $80 million. This means that the fund needs to earn a 25% return ($20 million out of $80 million) in order to earn back its management fee. For the median fund in a sample of 238 funds, Metrick and Yasuda (2010) calculate that lifetime management fees add up to 17.75% of committed capital for a VC fund and 12% for buyout. Using a larger sample of 837 funds, Robinson and Sensoy (2013) find 21.38% and 14.23%, respectively.

---

[3]This is received wisdom, but we are unaware of any explicit documentation of this point.

Table 2.2: Simplified example of a PE fund waterfall calculation. Negative numbers are cash outflows from capital calls and positive numbers are cash inflows from exits, in millions of dollars. The fictional fund has no management fee, 20% carried interest, an 8% hurdle rate, and 100% GP catch-up (see the text for a more detailed explanation of these terms). Carried interest is computed on a whole-fund basis (as opposed to deal-by-deal). The first four rows show the fund cash flows from the fund's investments in portfolio companies. The rows labeled "Hurdle" indicate the additional amount that must be returned to LPs in each year for each of the portfolio companies before the GP earns carried interest. The "Remaining hurdle" row shows the total hurdle amount that has not yet been returned to LPs by the end of the year

Year	0	1	2	3	4
Company A	−25	40			
Hurdle		2			
Company B	−25		60		
Hurdle		2	2.16		
Company C	−25			20	
Hurdle		2	2.16	2.33	
Company D	−25				30
Hurdle		2	2.16	2.33	2.52
Payoff to LPs	−100	40	60	19.15	20.85
Cumulative	−100	−60	0	19.15	40
Remaining hurdle	0	8	14.48	0	0
Payoff to GP	0	0	0	0.85	9.15
Cumulative	0	0	0	0.85	10

The second common fee charged by GPs is a profit share, most commonly equal to 20%, called "carried interest" or "carry". A GP starts to earn carry after the committed capital plus a hurdle rate (also known as "preferred return" or simply "pref") on outstanding investments has been returned to the LPs. Roughly half of VC funds and nearly all buyout funds have a hurdle rate (Metrick and Yasuda, 2010). For most funds with a hurdle, the rate is 8% per year, but there is some variation around this number. After the hurdle has been met, there is usually a "catch-up" in which the GP receives most or all of the cash flows until it reaches its carry payout of the fund's profits.

To see how the "waterfall" of payouts to LPs and GPs works out, consider the example of a fictitious $100 million fund as shown in Table 2.2. For simplicity, this fund has a portfolio of four companies, lasts for four years, and uses whole-fund carried interest. It does not charge a management fee, so the full $100 million is invested, and all investments are of equal size and assumed to take place upon fund inception (year 0). The fund has an 8% hurdle, 20% carry, and a 100% GP catch-up. Portfolio companies A and B are the first to experience exits, generating $40 and $60 million for the fund in year 1 and year 2, respectively. The full $100 million goes to the LPs, since the firm has not yet returned its called capital plus the hurdle, which by year 2 stands at $114.48 million ($100 million plus one year of hurdle on company A and two years of compounded 8% hurdle on the remaining portfolio companies B, C, and D). Next, company C has a $20 million exit in year 3. The first $19.15 million goes to the LPs to meet the hurdle, which has grown by another $4.66 million due to the investments in companies C and D. Under the catch-up arrangement the GP has the right to receive up to the next $4.8 million (based on $19.15 million paid-out fund profit times 20% divided by 80%). Therefore, the remaining $0.85 million from company C's exit is paid out as carry to the GP. Finally, by the end of year 4 the final portfolio company has exited, yielding $30 million, bringing total fund profits to date to $50 million. The GP receives $9.15 million from company D's exit to earn its 20% carry on the entire fund's profit, amounting to $10 million. This leaves $20.85 million for the LPs, for a cumulative payoff of $140 million, which is equal to committed capital plus their 80% profit share. Note that this puts the LP past the hurdle.

An alternative model to the whole-fund carried interest calculation of Table 2.2 is for carry to be paid on a deal-by-deal basis. As described in Hüther *et al.* (2020), "Historically, the timing of paying carried interest to general partners has followed one of two approaches. Deal-by-deal (DD) or 'American' ['GP friendly'] carry provisions allow the general partners to earn carried interest on each deal as it is exited, even if the fund as a whole has not returned sufficient capital to LPs for them to break even [usually combined with claw-backs]. Whole-fund (WF) or 'European' ['LP friendly'] carry provisions typically require that invested capital and fees are returned to LPs before the GP is entitled to earn any carried interest."[4]

A third set of fees, often used by buyout and real asset funds, are monitoring and transaction fees charged to portfolio companies for providing investment banking, management, and advisory services. Phalippou *et al.* (2018) observe that these "fees amount to $20 billion evenly distributed over time, representing over 6% of equity invested by GPs. They do not vary with business cycles, company characteristics, or GP performance." One reason for the lack of variation across cycles is that these fees represent rights that are written into the LPA and thus extend throughout the life of the fund. A fraction of these fees is generally kicked back to the LPs, often in the form of a reduction in management fees.

Figure 2.2 shows an example of what the net-of-fees cash flow stream of a fictitious fund might look like, from the perspective of an LP. Capital calls are negative cash flows and distributions are positive. Using real data, Figure 2.3 plots the average cumulative capital calls and distributions net-of-fees over a fund's life, normalized to a $10 million commitment, by asset class. It takes about three to five years to fully call the committed capital, while distributions start to ramp up when the fund is two to three years into its life cycle.

As is evident from Figure 2.3, many funds remain active beyond their initial 10-year life span. Per the LPA, the GP often has the option to extend the fund's life for another year or two, after which the LPs have to agree to any additional extensions, usually in yearly increments. When a fund still has investments that are yet to be exited, the usual solution is to extend the fund's life. A less common and less desired solution is to try to sell the portfolio companies to another GP, or, as a last resort, to distribute the shares in the portfolio companies directly to the LPs. Extensions have become more common in VC, as the time to exit has grown longer since the turn of the millennium. For early-stage investments, it can now take over a decade for the VC firm to exit an investment. By contrast, buyout funds usually exit a

---

[4]The whole-fund distribution of carry resembles high-water marks, which are often used by hedge funds to determine performance fees. High-water marks are not used in PE.

Net cash flow
to LP

Figure 2.2: Example of a PE fund cash flow pattern. Example of the net cash flow pattern over a fictitious PE fund's life, from a limited partner (LP) perspective. Cash flows are after fees. Distributions to the LP are positive cash flows. Capital calls by the fund are negative cash flows because they are outflows to the LP.

deal in three to seven years, and some portfolio companies generate intermediate income from dividends. Real estate funds also tend to have lower duration as intermediate cash flows are generated from property rental income. There have been some attempts at innovation on this front, with some GPs raising longer-duration vehicles, and a few firms have turned into publicly traded evergreen funds.

2.2.2 Implicit Incentives

Two stylized facts are particularly important in understanding the incentives created by the GP fee structure. First, most expected compensation comes from the fixed components of fees. From Metrick and Yasuda (2010), "about two-thirds of expected revenue comes from fixed-revenue components [fees] that are not sensitive to performance".

Second, the impact of current investments on future fundraising is as important as their impact on fees today. Since most of a GP's work is done during the investment period, GPs start raising their next fund near the tail end of this period, typically two to three years into the current fund. In fact, the LPA usually prevents them from raising

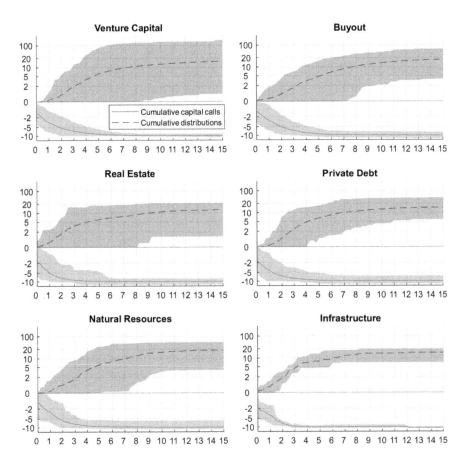

Figure 2.3: Cumulative cash flow patterns for PE asset classes. Average cumulative capital calls (red solid line) and distributions (blue striped line) for private equity funds with a North American geographic focus, by asset class. Funds of funds, secondary funds, co-investments, and venture debt funds are excluded. Cash flows are scaled to a $10 million commitment, and they are net of fees paid by the limited partners to the PE firm. Capital calls are shown as negative numbers because they are outflows to the LP. The horizontal axis is time since fund inception in years. The vertical axis is the cumulative cash flow in millions of dollars, on a logarithmic scale. The shaded areas show the 5th to 95th percentile range.
Source: Preqin.

a new fund before the current fund is close to fully invested; agency problems would explain why LPs would want to prevent a GP from investing simultaneously out of two separate funds. As a result, at any one time GPs usually have two or three active funds that are in different stages of their life cycle. Chung *et al.* (2012) show that indirect pay for performance from future funds is of similar magnitude as the pay for performance from the current fund's carried interest. As such, GPs face strong incentives from the market-based, implicit contract associated with future fundraising. These incentives are an important consideration throughout the monograph.

In addition, understanding the different incentives provided by whole-fund and deal-by-deal carried interest compensation is an active area of research. Hüther *et al.* (2020) conclude that the trade-off is between incentives for the GP and insurance for the LP: "Deal-by-deal provisions offer sharper incentives ... but their reliance on ex post settling up through clawbacks leaves the LP exposed to under-performance", while "whole-fund contracts protect LPs against under-performance but potentially blunt the incentives of GPs by allowing past exits to create a 'debt overhang problem' that may undermine the effort incentives in an ongoing investment". In a small sample, they find that GP-friendly contracts are associated with better net-of-fee performance. Rezaei (2020) points out the important role of correlation across portfolio companies when assessing DD or WF fee structures. If deal outcomes are highly correlated, bundling payouts together can enhance incentives, but DD contracts likely provide better incentives to weed bad projects out of an uncorrelated set.

2.3 Secondary Markets

The secondary market allows LPs to sell stakes in PE funds, enabling LPs to rebalance their portfolios or relieve themselves of future capital calls. This market has seen strong growth since the turn of the millennium, from a transaction volume of $2 billion in 2001 to $42 billion in 2014 (Nadauld *et al.*, 2019). Activity jumped up during the financial crisis of 2008, as many LPs found themselves with an excessive allocation to PE (in part due to the "denominator effect" of the drop in value in public equities) and liquidity concerns with respect to future capital calls. At the same time, transaction prices dropped precipitously during the crisis years, with average discounts to fund net asset values (NAVs) in 2009 as high as 46% (Nadauld *et al.*, 2019). Still, growth in secondary market sales continued after the crisis passed, and average discounts dropped to 7% of NAV by 2014. Despite its recent growth, the market is still illiquid, transaction costs are high, discounts are still sizeable, and it can take three to six months to complete a sale. Moreover, the GP usually has the right to veto a sale. Section 6 dives deeper into the secondary market and its implications for portfolio allocation.

Recently, there has been an increase in the purchase and sale of minority ownership claims on GP management companies. These GP stakes are essentially claims on the management and performance fees (carry and other fees) earned by the GP, and are usually passive and non-voting. GP stakes may be sold to large LPs; for example, Mubadala (an Abu Dhabi sovereign wealth fund) bought a 5% stake in Silver Lake in 2020. There are also funds that are set up explicitly to invest in GP stakes, such as Petershill and Dyal Capital. Finally, some large management companies are publicly listed, such as KKR and Blackstone.[5] These sales create agency concerns because they reduce a GP's skin-in-the-game, similar to the issues that arise when banks sell the equity tranches of mortgage backed securities (e.g., Demiroglu and James, 2012). The importance of this phenomenon in PE has not yet been explored.

Open Question 1: How common are sales of GP stakes, and how do they affect incentives and LP cash flows?
How frequently do sales of a stake in the GP management company occur? What are the descriptive characteristics of these sales (in terms of size, cash flow and control characteristics, etc.)? How strongly do they affect the selling GP's incentives? How do they impact calls and distributions for LPs?

---

[5]While the vast majority of PE funds are private, there are a few publicly traded PE funds and firms (Jegadeesh *et al.*, 2015; McCourt, 2018). These represent a relatively small and selected subsample, and they cannot be directly compared to the private PE funds. Some are a combination of GP and LP payoffs (e.g., Blackstone and KKR), whereas others are business development companies (BDCs) that tend to invest in high-yield corporate loans. As such, for the purpose of this monograph, we do not consider them as a primary way to gain PE exposure.

2.4   Co-Investments, Solo LP Investments, and Alternative Vehicles

Sometimes GPs offer select LPs the opportunity to invest in alternative vehicles to the main PE fund. Potential benefits from doing so are preferential access to high-quality deals or a reduction in the fees paid to the GP. Alternative PE investments of this kind have grown in prominence in recent years, from less than 10% of all capital invested in PE in the 1980s to almost 40% by 2017 (Lerner *et al.*, 2022). These alternative vehicles can be broadly categorized as discretionary vehicles or GP-directed vehicles. With discretionary vehicles, the GP offers opportunities to the LP, who can decide on a deal-by-deal basis whether or not to invest. These vehicles include co-investment funds. With GP-directed funds, the LPs have no decision power over individual deals. These funds tend to invest in similar deals to the GP's main fund.

Some LPs also pursue solo investments in PE deals to avoid GP fees altogether (Fang *et al.*, 2015). Doing so requires a sizeable PE team in order to generate deal flow and perform due diligence, even more so than discretionary funds where deal flow is generated by the GP. As such, this activity is primarily the domain of large investors.

We return to these alternative investment opportunities in Section 5.

3

Modern Portfolio Theory and Private Equity

There is no fully developed portfolio choice theory geared to fit all the specifics of PE, so this section begins by applying a simple version of Modern Portfolio Theory (MPT) to LP investment in private equity. We then illustrate MPT's shortcomings with respect to the institutional details of PE, and these shortcomings will motivate some of the open questions we describe later in the review.

Some of the problems with MPT appear to be familiar from other asset classes. For example, as with other illiquid assets, private equity funds are not traded, so the frequent prices that are needed to estimate risk structures are missing. However, there is usually a private equity twist. In the case of infrequent prices, the GP has an incentive to selectively report underlying values in a way that makes them look better; thus asset values are not just infrequently observed, they are selected due to an agency problem.

Other problems are simply outside the traditional framework of MPT. For example, LPs and GPs match in a market where both parties have pricing and bargaining power. The parties are not price takers; they act strategically. In another example, the fact that GPs have discretion over investment timing implies that LPs do not control the timing or the quantity of their investment.

To proceed, we first present a brief review of the classic portfolio choice problem first introduced into the literature by Markowitz (1952), followed by an empirical exercise in which we attempt to implement the MPT solution. Then, with that structure laid out, we spend the rest of the monograph detailing the consequences of the particularities of private equity.

3.1   Theory

Assume an investor has mean-variance preferences over the return on their total portfolio (wealth) over the next period, R_p, as expressed by the expected utility function

$$E[U(R_p)] = E[R_p] - \frac{\gamma}{2}V[R_p], \qquad (3.1)$$

where $E[R_p]$ and $V[R_p]$ are the mean and variance of the portfolio return, and $\gamma > 0$ is a risk-aversion coefficient that indicates how strongly the investor dislikes variance. This utility function implies that the investor prefers a higher expected return for a given level of variance or a lower variance given an expected return. If γ were equal to zero, then the investor would be risk-neutral and would only care about the expected return of their portfolio irrespective of the amount of risk taken; we do not consider the risk-neutral case as it is not empirically relevant for the investors we are concerned with.

The portfolio consists of a riskless security with return R_f and $i = 1, \ldots, N$ risky securities, each with its own return, R_i. Let w_i denote the dollar investment in each risky security as a fraction of the total portfolio value (portfolio weights), and define the (column) vectors $R = [R_1, \ldots, R_N]'$ and $w = [w_1, \ldots, w_N]'$ to be the collection of returns and portfolio weights, respectively. Label the dollar fraction of the portfolio invested in the riskless security as w_0. Then portfolio weights sum to one: $w_0 + \mathbf{1}'w = 1$, where $\mathbf{1}$ is a N-by-1 vector of ones.[1] The

---

[1]If borrowing is allowed, then w_0 can be negative and $\mathbf{1}'w$ greater than one. Conversely, if short-sales are allowed then $\mathbf{1}'w$ can be negative and w_0 greater than one.

riskless security is considered separately from the risky assets because its variance is zero. The vector of securities' excess returns is $R_e \equiv R - 1R_f$. The portfolio return is then

$$R_p = w_0 R_f + w'R = w_0 R_f + w'(1R_f + R_e) = R_f + w'R_e. \qquad (3.2)$$

Define μ to be the vector of risky-asset expected excess returns ($\mu = E[R_e] = E[R - 1R_f]$) and Σ to be the corresponding variance-covariance matrix ($\Sigma = V[R_e]$). From equation (3.2), the excess return on the portfolio is $\mu_P = E[R_p] - R_f = w'\mu$. The portfolio's expected return and variance are

$$E[R_p] = R_f + w'\mu, \qquad (3.3)$$
$$V[R_p] = w'\Sigma w. \qquad (3.4)$$

The investor's problem is to choose the portfolio weights to maximize expected utility

$$\max_w E[U(R_p)] = \max_w R_f + w'\mu - \frac{\gamma}{2}w'\Sigma w. \qquad (3.5)$$

Solving for the optimal weights (w^*) yields the first-order condition $\mu - \gamma\Sigma w^* = 0$ and solution

$$w^* = \frac{1}{\gamma}\Sigma^{-1}\mu. \qquad (3.6)$$

This solution is intuitively appealing. First, the higher the expected excess return on a particular security, the more weight the investor places on that security, all else equal. Second, if all securities are uncorrelated (that is, Σ is a diagonal matrix), each security's optimal weight is proportional to the ratio of its mean excess return to its variance.[2] Third, the higher the risk-aversion coefficient (γ), the lower the weight the investor places on each of the N risky assets and the higher the weight placed on the riskless asset. The allocation to the riskless security can be found from $w_0 = 1 - 1'w^*$. Finally, in the optimal portfolio, $\mu_p/V[R_p] = \gamma$, which is simply another way of representing the intuition

---

[2] An equivalent way of phrasing this result is to say that if all security returns are uncorrelated, then each security's risk weight, $\sigma_i w_i$, is proportional to its Sharpe ratio.

that a more risk-averse investor requires a higher expected excess return for a given level of variance.

The model is more general than the determination of allocations to individual securities (e.g., single stocks or venture capital funds). For example, "securities" can be portfolios themselves, from broad asset classes (such as public stocks, corporate bonds, or private equity) to mutual funds or individual timber holdings. Similarly, we can think of the allocation problem from the perspective of the entire investor's portfolio (across all possible investments) or within the private equity space (tackling the question of how to allocate a given PE budget to various strategies and funds).[3]

Besides its simplicity and intuition, the portfolio allocation model also has a natural connection to factor pricing models, in particular the Capital Asset Pricing Model (CAPM). To see this, we consider an alternate portfolio that adds a small weight, ξ, of security i to the investor's current portfolio. This security could already be in the portfolio, in which case it simply gets a higher weight at the expense of all other securities, or it could be a new security. The alternate portfolio's excess return and its variance are

$$\mu_{p'} = \xi\mu_i + (1 - \xi)\mu_p \tag{3.7}$$
$$V[R_{p'}] = \xi^2 V[R_i] + (1 - \xi)^2 V[R_p] + 2\xi(1 - \xi)Cov[R_i, R_p]. \tag{3.8}$$

If the original portfolio was chosen optimally, then the derivative of (3.1) with respect to ξ should be zero at $\xi = 0$, which yields $\mu_i - \mu_p + \gamma V[R_p] - \gamma Cov[R_i, R_p] = 0$. Since $\gamma = \mu_p/V[R_p]$ (from 3.6), we obtain

$$\mu_i = \beta_i \mu_p, \tag{3.9}$$

with $\beta_i \equiv Cov[R_i, R_p]/V[R_p]$. Thus, the expected excess return on an individual security equals its beta with the investor's portfolio times the expected excess return on the portfolio. This is true of any security in any existing portfolio that has been chosen optimally. If instead, we

---

[3]However, it is not the case that a two-step procedure of first choosing a PE portfolio and then mixing it with other assets will generate the same outcome as choosing all assets simultaneously. See, for example, Sharpe (1981) or Van Binsbergen *et al.* (2008).

observe an inequality

$$\mu_i \gtrless \beta_i \mu_p, \tag{3.10}$$

then the allocation to the asset should be increased ($>$) or reduced ($<$) until equality holds.

To specialize the result and obtain the CAPM, one can assume that all investors have the same information and opportunity set and therefore choose the same portfolio. Since all securities have to be owned in equilibrium, the portfolio P has to be the market portfolio, that is, $R_p = R_M$. The CAPM follows.

3.2 An Empirical Application

To illustrate the mean-variance solution, suppose our investor wants to allocate their portfolio across broad asset classes, specifically, public stocks, bonds, real estate, and PE. Given the structure of the PE industry described in Section 2, this is not a trivial exercise, and in order to illustrate a naive approach, this section ignores many of the issues that will be discussed in later sections.

The immediate issue that arises is how to compute a series of returns for a portfolio of PE funds at regular intervals when there are no regularly observed fund market prices. A solution that appears intuitive at first pass is to use fund net asset values (NAVs) as a substitute for market values, since GPs report fund NAVs to LPs on a quarterly basis. Leaving a discussion of the relation between NAVs and market prices for later (see Section 4.1), we can now compute an aggregate ("pooled") quarterly return using aggregate NAVs, NAV_t, and aggregate net cash flows (distributions minus capital calls), C_t, summed across funds in the same quarter, t,

$$R_t = \frac{NAV_t + C_t}{NAV_{t-1}}. \tag{3.11}$$

Note that this is the value-weighted return on a portfolio of funds, with weights that are proportional to the constituent funds' NAVs. Cambridge Associates, a large investment firm that provides portfolio management and advisory services to many LPs, uses this type of calculation to produce a benchmark return series for venture capital and buyout, which is freely available to the public.[4]

For stock returns, we use the Vanguard Total Stock Market Index Fund (mutual fund code VITSX), which closely tracks the CRSP U.S. value-weighted stock index. Our bond fund is the Vanguard Total Bond Market Index Fund (VBTIX), a portfolio of investment-grade U.S. Treasuries and mortgage-backed securities of all maturities that very closely replicates the Bloomberg Barclays U.S. Aggregate Bond Index. For real estate, we use the Dimensional Fund Advisors Real Estate Securities Portfolio (DFREX), which primarily invests in residential and commercial real estate investment trusts (REITs). Since most LPs are institutions, we use the institutional share classes of these funds. For the risk-free rate we use the three-month U.S. Treasury bill. We have return data on all assets for the 90 quarters ranging from the fourth quarter of 1997 until the first quarter of 2020, but we lose the first two quarters in the unsmoothing exercise described in Section 4.1.1, leaving us with a sample period of 88 quarters.

Table 3.1 reports descriptive statistics. Panel A shows that the stock index had an average annualized return of 7.58% and a standard deviation of 17.67%. Its Sharpe ratio, the ratio of its mean return in excess of the risk-free rate to its standard deviation, is 0.32. Bonds performed well during this sample period, with a mean (standard deviation) of 4.89% (3.41%) and a Sharpe ratio of 0.90. Real estate performed similarly to stocks, with a few percentage point higher mean and standard deviation, and a slightly higher Sharpe ratio. VC, as reported by Cambridge Associates, had a 13.60% annualized average return, which is higher than any other asset class over this period, but also experienced a higher standard deviation, of 24.42% per year. Still, its Sharpe ratio appeared quite high at 0.48. Buyout had an average return of 11.65%, about 1.5 percentage points above real estate but at only about half its volatility, for a Sharpe ratio that appears

---

[4]It is not entirely clear from their description how the benchmark return series is calculated, but we have compared the Cambridge Associates buyout benchmark returns with returns computed from buyout fund data from Burgiss (another large LP advisory firm) using Equation (3.11), and found an 86% correlation. Any differences are most likely due to differences in PE fund coverage between the two firms.

Table 3.1: Descriptive statistics of returns by asset class. This table reports descriptive statistics for quarterly asset class returns from the second quarter of 1998 until the first quarter of 2020. "Stocks" is the Vanguard Total Stock Market Index Fund (VITSX), "Bonds" is the Vanguard Total Bond Market Index Fund (VBTIX), and "Real Estate" is the Dimensional Fund Advisors Real Estate Securities Portfolio (DFREX). All stock, bond, and real estate fund returns are for institutional share classes. For "VC" and "Buyout" we use the Cambridge Associates U.S. Venture Capital and U.S. Private Equity benchmark returns, respectively. The columns labeled "Original" use the returns as reported by Cambridge Associates. The "Unsmoothed" columns are calculated using the unsmoothing algorithm of Geltner (1991) using two lags of the return series. Panel A shows descriptive statistics of annualized returns, where a return of 1.00 stands for 1% per year. "Exc. Kurtosis" is the excess kurtosis of the return distribution relative to the Normal distribution. Panel B shows correlations of contemporaneous quarterly returns across asset classes. Panel C reports the first four lags of autocorrelations in quarterly returns

	Stocks	Bonds	Real Estate	Original VC	Original Buyout	Unsmoothed VC	Unsmoothed Buyout
Panel A: Descriptive Statistics of Annualized Returns							
Mean	7.58	4.89	10.20	13.60	11.65	12.26	10.04
St.Dev	17.67	3.41	20.95	24.42	10.51	64.96	25.91
Skewness	−0.28	−0.06	−0.39	1.82	−0.25	1.27	−0.19
Exc. Kurtosis	0.08	−0.14	0.91	5.35	0.52	4.79	0.32
Percentile:							
25th	−7.58	−0.04	−7.98	−0.90	1.42	−25.30	−13.17
50th	11.60	5.02	10.36	9.56	15.10	14.17	12.90
75th	25.42	10.12	35.26	21.48	21.12	44.30	32.06
Sharpe ratio	0.32	0.90	0.40	0.48	0.93	0.16	0.31
Panel B: Correlations							
Stocks	1.00	−0.39	0.62	0.42	0.79	0.51	0.82
Bonds		1.00	0.02	−0.27	−0.41	−0.32	−0.39
Real Estate			1.00	0.08	0.47	0.10	0.46
VC – Original				1.00	0.64	0.76	0.49
Buyout – Original					1.00	0.55	0.87
VC – Unsmoothed						1.00	0.62
Buyout – Unsmoothed							1.00
Panel C: Autocorrelations							
1 quarter	−0.04	0.05	0.12	0.61	0.33	−0.00	−0.05
2 quarters	0.03	−0.07	−0.18	0.49	0.29	0.09	−0.05
3 quarters	−0.07	0.01	−0.08	0.31	0.10	0.15	−0.07
4 quarters	−0.05	−0.03	−0.05	0.02	0.04	−0.24	−0.04

Table 3.2: Normalized mean-variance portfolio weights. Portfolio weights for a mean-variance investor, with risk asset weights (w^* in Section 3.1) normalized to sum to one. The asset classes are as described in Table 3.1. The columns represent different investment opportunity sets, with blank cells indicating assets that are not part of the set

	(1)	(2)	(3)	(4)	(5)	(6)	(7)
Stocks	0.12	0.06	−0.07	−0.07	0.10	0.08	0.07
Bonds	0.90	0.87	0.74	0.73	0.90	0.91	0.91
Real Estate	−0.02	−0.00	−0.02	−0.03	−0.02	−0.02	−0.02
VC – Original		0.07		−0.02			
Buyout – Original			0.36	0.38			
VC – Unsmoothed					0.01		0.00
Buyout – Unsmoothed						0.04	0.03

impressively high at 0.93. Panel B reports contemporaneous return correlations, which reveal some noteworthy patterns. The correlation of stocks and bonds is quite strongly negative, at −0.39, whereas real estate is highly correlated with stocks (0.62) but virtually uncorrelated with bonds. VC and especially buyout correlate quite strongly with stocks (0.42 and 0.79, respectively), and negatively with bonds (−0.27 and −0.41). VC does not have any mentionable correlation with real estate, but buyout comoves fairly strongly with it, with a correlation coefficient of 0.47. Finally, the correlation between VC and buyout is 0.64.

Our mean-variance investor optimally allocates portfolio weights as reported in Table 3.2. To highlight the differences in relative weights among the assets, we show $\frac{w^*}{1'w^*}$, that is, the optimal weights on risky assets from Equation (3.6), normalized to sum to one. These weights are independent of the investor's level of risk aversion (γ), which drives the allocation to the riskless asset (or leverage, if $w_0 < 0$), but not the relative allocations between the risky assets. The first column in Table 3.2 shows the allocation among the publicly traded assets, ignoring PE as an investment opportunity. It is not surprising that bonds receive a 90% weight given their performance over the sample period. Despite its decent Sharpe ratio, real estate gets a virtually zero allocation. Instead, the investor favors stocks, which are positively correlated with real estate but with better hedging properties with bonds. Column 2 shows that some of the stock and bond position is reallocated to create a 7% weight on VC when that opportunity is added as an option.[5] Including buyout (instead of VC) results in a much larger allocation of 36% (column 3). Column 4 shows that adding both VC and buyout to the investment opportunity set results in an almost identical allocation to buyout, with VC receiving effectively no weight.

3.3   Problems with Mean-Variance Applications in PE

If the assumptions behind the mean-variance model are true *and* if PE portfolio returns from Equation (3.11) are achievable, then our story would end here. Unfortunately, neither condition holds. We organize the rest of the monograph around three core conceptual problems with the MPT approach as implemented above. First (Section 4), performance is very difficult to measure, both at the level of the PE industry and at the level of individual funds. There is no investable index of private equity, and fund level returns are beset by manipulation and selection. Second (Section 5), LP–GP matches are the outcome of a strategic game, and LPs experience persistent return differences related to their characteristics and goals. Third (Section 6), constructing a portfolio of private equity investments requires diversification across funds within a given vintage year and across time. Cyclical market conditions and GP discretion individually and jointly act to confound the usual diversification techniques.

---

[5]Chen *et al.* (2002) also find an optimal VC allocation of 9% in a mean-variance portfolio application looking only at stocks and VC, and using different data and a different methodology for computing returns.

4

Performance Measurement

The return properties of investible assets are a primary input into any portfolio allocation exercise. In this section we discuss the problems that arise in measuring PE returns and GP performance. We illustrate the significant difficulties at both the asset class and the fund level, and we summarize the literature on the risk exposures of PE. We briefly review the current state of knowledge regarding risk-adjusted returns estimates (other recent surveys, including Korteweg, 2019 and Kaplan and Sensoy, 2015, review this topic in detail). Each subsection moves from the existing literature to gaps in the literature and open questions.

4.1 Industry-Level Performance

Industry-level PE returns are often used as a performance benchmark. We first discuss measurement issues for aggregate returns, and then review the literature on risk factor loadings for PE asset classes.

4.1.1 Measuring Aggregate Performance

A key issue with measuring returns in PE, including the Cambridge Associates index we used in Section 3.2, is that market prices are not regularly observed and net asset values (NAVs) are commonly used as an alternative, as in Equation (3.11). However, not all GPs report their fund NAVs at the end of the calendar quarter: Some report in January, April, July, and October, others in February, May, etc. This induces a small amount of staleness into the index. A much larger degree of staleness enters due to typically conservative updating of the value of portfolio positions. Even though Accounting Standards Code (ASC) Topic 820 (formerly known as FAS 157) requires the fair valuation of portfolio companies starting in 2007, there is no market to which to mark Level 3 assets such as private equity portfolio investments. GPs (or their consultants) and auditors often rely on the pricing of recent deals and valuations of comparable assets. This process is subjective, and many GPs lean toward conservatism, marking asset values up slowly while being more aggressive in marking them down if they think their value has dropped (Anson, 2002, 2007).

If NAVs are stale, then the aggregate observed NAV is a mix of current and past market values. The resulting observed NAV series behaves like a moving average, that is, a smoothed representation of the true fundamental value process. Staleness creates autocorrelation in observed returns, downward biased estimates of fundamental return volatility, and downward biased estimates of risk factor loadings (see, for example, Korteweg, 2022 for a more detailed description). As an indicator of the magnitude of this issue, note that the first-order autocorrelations in quarterly VC and buyout returns in Panel C of Table 3.1 are 0.61 and 0.33, respectively, compared to near-zero autocorrelations of stocks, bonds, and (traded) real estate. This smoothing problem has been long recognized in the real estate literature, where appraisal-based index returns are subject to the same staleness concerns, and it also shows up in other asset classes, such as hedge funds. Numerous unsmoothing algorithms have been proposed (e.g., Couts *et al.*, 2020; Fisher *et al.*, 1994; Geltner, 1991, 1993; Getmansky *et al.*, 2004). For applications in private equity, see Goetzmann *et al.* (2019), Brown *et al.* (2020b), and Aliaga-Díaz *et al.* (2020).

To illustrate the effect of unsmoothing on returns and portfolio allocations, we use the Geltner (1991) algorithm in the mean-variance choice problem of the previous section. Assume that observed returns,

R_t, are a weighted average of the current fundamental return, R_t^*, and its prior p realizations,

$$R_t = \theta_0 R_t^* + \theta(L) R_{t-1}^*, \qquad (4.1)$$

where $\theta(L) = \theta_1 + \theta_2 L + \cdots + \theta_p L^{p-1}$ and L is the lag operator, such that $L^s R_t = R_{t-s}$. The θ's are all fractions between zero and one, and they sum to one. Equation (4.1) implies that the observed return also follows an autoregressive process,

$$R_t = \phi(L) R_{t-1} + e_t, \qquad (4.2)$$

with the error term $e_t = \theta_0 R_t^*$. In theory, (4.2) is an infinite-order autoregressive process, i.e., $\Phi(L) = \Phi_1 + \Phi_2 L + \Phi_3 L^2 + \cdots$, but if $\theta_0 > \theta_p$ for all $p > 0$, the higher-order lags tend to vanish quickly. To recover R^*, invert Equation (4.2):

$$R_t^* = (R_t - \phi(L) R_{t-1})/\theta_0. \qquad (4.3)$$

The Φ coefficients can be estimated from (4.2), but this leaves θ_0 unidentified. Two common solutions are to choose θ_0 to either equate the mean return of the reported and unsmoothed series (such that $\theta_0 = 1 - \sum_j \Phi_j$ using all j lags in Equation (4.2)), or to calibrate the volatility of the unsmoothed series to a specific number (Geltner *et al.*, 2003). The true means of the two series have to be equal since the θ's in (4.1) sum to one, although this is not necessarily true for average returns in finite samples. The volatility-matching alternative is ad-hoc, and there is little guidance regarding what volatility to calibrate to. Fortunately, for mean-variance portfolio weights, the choice of θ_0 is not crucial: since it is merely a scaling constant, means and standard deviations remain proportional to each other, and skewness, kurtosis, autocorrelations and correlations with other assets remain identical irrespective of the value of θ_0. With Sharpe ratios little affected by the choice of θ_0, the resulting mean-variance portfolio weights are also nearly unchanged.

Table 3.1 shows the descriptive statistics of the unsmoothed VC and buyout returns from the Cambridge Associates returns, with 2 quarter lags in the autoregression model (4.2), and equating mean returns to determine θ_0. The average return of the unsmoothed VC and buyout series are 12.26% and 10.04%, close to that of the reported data (13.60% and 11.65%), by construction. As expected, volatility is substantially higher, at 64.96% per year for VC (compared to 24.42% in the reported data) and 25.91% for buyout (compared to 10.51%). Not surprisingly, unsmoothing lowers the Sharpe ratios quite dramatically, from 0.48 to 0.16 for VC, and from 0.93 to 0.31 for buyout. Skewness and excess kurtosis of the unsmoothed returns are slightly closer to zero, but remain substantial, especially for VC. Panel B shows that the unsmoothed and reported returns have a high correlation coefficient of 0.76 for VC and 0.87 for buyout, and they have similar correlations with other asset returns. Finally, Panel C shows that smoothing virtually eliminates the autocorrelation in the return series, as it is designed to do.[1]

Table 3.2, columns 5 through 7, show the mean-variance portfolio weights calculated using the unsmoothed PE returns. Not surprising, given the lower Sharpe ratios, the PE weights are much lower than those for the reported returns in columns 2 through 4. Both VC and buyout now get weights close to zero, a difference that is especially striking for buyout.

The zero portfolio weight result should be taken with some skepticism. The assumption that the fundamental values produce a return series with no autocorrelation is plausible in a setting in which the efficient market hypothesis is likely to hold (at the risk of oversimplification, liquid markets with low transaction costs). But in the illiquid private equity market there is no reason to presume this is true. Some unsmoothing algorithms allow for autocorrelation in the unsmoothed return series, such as Geltner (1993), but these have drawbacks of their own, and often rely on assumptions that are rather subjective.

---

[1]For comparison, we also implemented the alternative approach to fix θ_0, calibrating the volatility of the unsmoothed return series to match the VC and buyout index volatility estimates in Ang *et al.* (2018), Table IV. For VC, this results in an annualized mean return of 6.65% and a volatility of 35.27%, nearly half the numbers as shown in Table 3.1. The mean and volatility of buyout are virtually unchanged, at 10.25% and 26.45%. As mentioned above, higher moments, and (auto)correlations are identical to those in Tables 3.1 and 3.2. Sharpe ratios and portfolio weights are virtually unchanged. We do not report the full results for brevity.

It is also not clear what is the micro-foundation of Equation (4.1). The capital gain part of the index return can be made to fit this equation using a stale price setup in the spirit of Dimson (1979), with each constituent fund's NAV having a certain probability of being updated to its true fundamental value in each period.[2] However, the cash flow component of the return is not stale, i.e., contributions and distributions are observed for the quarter in which they occur. To make the Dimson setup work, one would have to get to a linear specification like (4.1) by using a log-linear approximation of observed returns (along the lines of Campbell and Shiller, 1988) to separate the capital gain and the cash yield component of the return. Since most readily available indices (such as Cambridge Associates) only report returns and do not distinguish capital gain and cash yield, such a decomposition cannot be readily implemented.

Other proposals to deal with price staleness include using longer-horizon returns, the Dimson (1979) method of using leads and lags to estimate (co-)variances, imputation or filtering of valuations, and using secondary market prices.

The logic behind using longer-horizon returns, suggested by Emery (2003), is that there is more time for NAVs to adjust to fundamental values. Drawbacks are that the time series of PE returns is short to begin with, and – unlike averages – lower frequency data results in less precise estimates of (co)variances. It could be helpful to use overlapping observations (with a correction to account for serial correlation, for example, Hansen and Hodrick, 1980), but we haven't found an application of this in the literature.

The Dimson (1979) approach was developed to estimate factor loadings (such as CAPM betas) in the presence of staleness, by adding leads and lags of the risk factors to the regression model and summing the resulting factor loadings across all leads and lags. Since commonly used risk factors are not stale themselves, it suffices to include only lags (and no leads) of the factors. Examples of applications in PE are

---

[2]The issue can be further complicated by recognizing that a fund itself is a portfolio of investments, each of which is updated to true fundamental values with some probability. Thus, fund-level regressions that rely on NAVs are subject to very similar staleness concerns.

Anson (2007), Ewens *et al.* (2013), Peters (2018), Woodward (2009). This method could be adapted to estimate covariances to feed into a portfolio allocation problem.

Gompers and Lerner (1997) propose a method to impute market values by taking the most recently observed values for portfolio companies (for example, from a start-up's financing round) and multiplying them by the return to an index of publicly traded firms in the same three-digit SIC industry from the observation dates until the present period. A disadvantage of this approach is that it requires data on portfolio investments that is usually not available for fund-level data sets.[3] Further complicating the issue, estimates of means, (co)variances, and factor loadings would need to account for the estimation error in imputing valuations, but this is often ignored. (This issue also underscores the problem with the portfolio theory assumption of known means and covariances.) Brown *et al.* (2020a) instead specify a state-space model in order to filter unobserved fund NAVs that does not require investment-level data. They report that the annual standard deviation of a median venture (buyout) fund is 13 (10) percentage points higher compared to estimates based on as-reported NAVs.

Finally, Boyer *et al.* (2018) use secondary market prices from sales in LP stakes instead of NAVs to estimate risk factor loadings. This method is closest to using actual fundamental fund values but is hampered by the illiquidity of the secondary market.

Besides staleness, NAVs suffer from three additional problems that make them unreliable measures of value. First, GPs can strategically manipulate NAVs (see Section 4.2.3 for more detail). Second, NAVs are reported on a pre-fee (in particular, pre-carried interest) basis. The third problem is specific to VC, where fund NAVs are often based on the post-money valuations of portfolio companies' most recent funding rounds (or those of similar companies). Post-money values implicitly assume that all investors own the same type of security. This is not the

---

[3]It is also possible to construct index returns directly from investment-level data (see, for example, Peng, 2001 and Hwang *et al.*, 2005 for venture capital). This skips the fund-level data altogether, but unobserved valuations still need to be imputed. Moreover, this approach introduces new sample selection concerns, such as survivorship bias not present in (liquidated) funds data.

case, as VCs typically own preferred stock (with terms that vary from round to round) whereas founders and employees own common stock. As a result, post-money valuations tend to be biased upwards relative to true fundamental value (Ewens *et al.*, 2022; Gornall and Strebulaev, 2020; Metrick and Yasuda, 2010).

None of the staleness solutions were devised to deal with these additional problems. Secondary market prices may do a good job controlling for most of these concerns, while imputation and filtering methods may be able to handle the NAV manipulation problem (and longer-horizon returns may mitigate it). However, the efficacy of these techniques remains an open question.

Open Question 2: How are various staleness correction methods impacted by NAV manipulation, fees, and post-money valuations?
To what extent are staleness correction methods for PE returns (unsmoothing, long-horizon returns, the Dimson (1979) correction, imputation or filtering of NAVs, and using secondary market prices) affected by potential NAV manipulation by GPs, the mixing of pre and post fee data in NAVs and cash flows, and the bias in post-money valuations in VC?

Open Question 3: What is the time-series process for fund NAVs, and what is its micro-foundation?
How are reported fund NAVs connected to fundamental values, and what are the time-series properties of both the (unobserved) fundamental process and the (observed) NAV process?

A final issue is that estimates of means and (co)variances for PE have a high level of uncertainty which creates unstable optimal portfolio positions across periods. While this is a concern for other asset classes as well, the problem is worse in PE given its short time series and the high volatility of returns, especially for VC. A common solution in other settings has been to apply some type of shrinkage estimator. Shrinkage goes back as far as Stein (1956) and can be applied both to estimates of means (e.g., Black and Litterman, 1990, 1992) and covariance matrices (e.g., Ledoit and Wolf, 2004). Separately, parameter uncertainty has a direct impact on portfolio weights, as it increases the volatility of perceived future returns, and it creates a role for learning about parameters, especially for long-horizon investors (e.g., Barberis, 2000; Brandt *et al.*, 2005; Brennan, 1998; Johannes *et al.*, 2014; Stambaugh, 1999; Xia, 2001). We are not aware of any work that considers the effects of PE parameter uncertainty on portfolio allocations:

Open Question 4: How should one correct for parameter uncertainty in PE allocations?

How much time-series variation in optimal PE portfolio weights is induced by parameter uncertainty? Are shrinkage methods effective in addressing this problem? How large is the effect of estimation risk on optimal portfolio weights?

4.1.2   Factor Loadings

A substantial and growing literature examines the risk loadings ("betas") and risk-adjusted return ("alpha") of PE investments, where alpha is defined as the difference between the security's expected return and its benchmark return based on its risk loadings. For example, the CAPM benchmark return is $\beta_i \mu_M$, based on Equation (3.9) and an aggregate stock market index M. A positive alpha is indicative of a return advantage (perhaps, for example, manager skill, which we discuss in Section 4.3), and such a security should receive a higher portfolio allocation.[4] In this section, we focus on factor loading estimates from the literature.

Korteweg (2019) reviews the literature on risk loadings and risk-adjusted returns in PE, and we refer the interested reader to that paper for a detailed discussion and additional references. Several stylized facts emerge, despite substantial variation in estimated factor loadings across

---

[4]We are ignoring the general equilibrium consideration that any precisely known alpha would be traded away, barring transaction costs. Instead, we focus on the fact that estimates of alpha are uncertain and that the risk structure of private equity is, as of now, not fully understood.

time periods, data sources, and methodologies. First, VC fund returns load highly on aggregate market returns, centered around a CAPM beta of 1.8 but with individual estimates as low as 0.9 and as high as 2.7. Buyout funds have considerably lower market risk, with the bulk of estimates concentrated around 1. Generally, buyout market betas range from 0.7 to 1.3.[5]

A number of papers consider the Fama and French three factor model, which expands the set of factors to include two additional risk factors. The first addition is a size factor, SMB, that represents the premium of small company returns over the return on large firms. The second addition is a value factor, HML, that captures the return premium to value stocks over growth stocks. VC typically loads positively on SMB and negatively on HML, indicating that they behave like small-growth stocks. Buyout funds do not have a consistent size loading but do load positively on HML. The value loading is indicative of the traditional buyout strategy of taking over struggling firms and turning them around. With the recent expansion of buyout into other strategies, including more early stage investments, these loadings may be weaker going forward.[6]

Empirical work on the size of a liquidity premium is still in its infancy. Franzoni *et al.* (2012) and Ang *et al.* (2018) find positive loadings of PE on the Pastor and Stambaugh (2003) liquidity factor for buyout, implying a liquidity premium of about 3% per year. Loadings for VC are insignificant. However, the Pastor and Stambaugh factor was developed to measure market microstructure (order flow-based) illiquidity. This is illiquidity of a different nature, and operates at a much higher frequency than the type of illiquidity that LPs are generally concerned about with

---

[5]Papers that estimate CAPM betas in private equity include Gompers and Lerner (1997); Peng (2001); Cochrane (2005); Hwang *et al.* (2005); Anson (2007); Woodward (2009); Korteweg and Sørensen (2010); Groh and Gottschalg (2011); Franzoni *et al.* (2012); Driessen *et al.* (2012); Ewens *et al.* (2013); Axelson *et al.* (2014); Buchner and Stucke (2014); Jegadeesh *et al.* (2015); Stafford (2022); Ang *et al.* (2018); Boyer *et al.* (2018); Peters (2018).

[6]Papers that estimate the Fama-French 3 factor model in PE include Gompers and Lerner (1997); Korteweg and Sørensen (2010); Driessen *et al.* (2012); Ewens *et al.* (2013); Ang *et al.* (2018); McCourt (2018); Peters (2018).

respect to their PE investments. We discuss the role of illiquidity in PE in more detail in Section 6 below.

Idiosyncratic risk could also be priced in PE. Since GPs are under-diversified, they may price their exposure to this type of risk into the contract they negotiate with portfolio companies (Ewens *et al.*, 2013; Opp, 2019). The small set of papers in this area has focused on VC, where idiosyncratic risk is highest. The empirical evidence is mixed. On the one hand, Opp (2019) finds only marginal effects of imperfect risk sharing on agents' marginal utility and investment dynamics in VC. On the other hand, in a survey of VCs, Gompers *et al.* (2020) find that 42% of VCs treat systematic and idiosyncratic risk the same way: 5% discount systematic risk more, and 14% discount idiosyncratic risk more. Ewens *et al.* (2013) find that VC funds with higher idiosyncratic risk earn higher average returns. In the time series, Peters (2018) finds that VC funds load positively and significantly on aggregate idiosyncratic risk shocks. Since such shocks have a negative risk price (meaning that investors like securities that pay off when idiosyncratic risk unexpectedly increases, see, e.g., Ang *et al.*, 2006), this reduces the expected return on VC. We discuss the role of idiosyncratic risk in the LP's diversification problem in more detail in Section 6.1.

Korteweg and Sørensen (2010) and Ang *et al.* (2018) present suggestive evidence of a factor that is specific to the private equity market. However, the nature of such a factor is as of yet unknown. A possible source in VC is the hedge that venture investments provide against aggregate downturns (Opp, 2019) or against displacement risk in public firms (Gârleanu *et al.*, 2012; Kogan *et al.*, 2020).

To summarize, the literature has only scratched the surface of the realm of possible risk factors in PE. Many other potential sources of risk, such as factors related to the term structure of interest rates (e.g., Gupta and Van Nieuwerburgh, 2020), need to be investigated in more depth or still remain to be discovered. There may also be a fair amount of heterogeneity in factor loadings across funds within the same strategy. Methods to estimate fund-specific loadings are on the frontier of the literature (e.g., Brown *et al.*, 2020a).

Open Question 5: What are the risk factors (and their loadings) for PE? Are there PE-specific factors?
Research has only just started to explore the set of risk factors and their loadings for private equity. What is the relevant set of factors that LPs should consider? Do the factors and their loadings differ across PE segments? Are there any PE or segment-specific risk factors?

Finally, the existence of factor models can be built on any one of multiple foundations, and the MPT discussion in Section 3.1 is one example. At present, however, it is not clear if there is a micro-foundation for factor models that fits the realities of PE:

Open Question 6: How valid is the use of factor models in PE?
There are multiple sets of sufficient conditions that will lead to factor models or factor-like models. Given the frictions in PE, such as required minimum capital commitments by LPs, infrequent fundraising by individual GPs, and an illiquid secondary market, are factor models valid for PE? If they are, what is the micro-foundation?

4.2 Fund-Level Performance

In Section 4.1, we considered the portfolio choice problem using broad asset class returns. However, investable indices of PE do not currently exist, so, either by choice or by force, LPs have to build portfolios of individual funds.[7] Thus, we turn to individual fund performance measurement. Fund-level return metrics are widely reported, and they are available in many commercial data sets; popular examples are Burgiss, Pitchbook, Preqin, and Thomson VentureXpert (formerly Thomson Venture Economics). Popular performance metrics summarize the performance for the fund since inception in one number, relying as much as

---

[7]LPs could invest in funds of funds or secondary funds, which are portfolios of funds, at the cost of an extra layer of fees. Regardless, a fund-of-funds faces a similar portfolio choice problem as the one described here.

possible on fund cash flows. While a quarterly return series at the fund level could be constructed using a calculation similar to Equation (3.11), such returns are not commonly used or reported at the fund level, presumably due to the issues with NAVs described above.

4.2.1 Common Performance Measures

Two performance measures for private equity funds are widely used in practice as well as in the academic literature: Total Value to Paid-In Capital Multiple (TVPI) and internal rate of return (IRR).[8] TVPI is a cash multiple, equal to total fund distributions to date, divided by the sum of capital calls.[9] IRR is a textbook measure of returns that is used across many investment settings. In the PE space, IRR is computed as the discount rate that, when applied to fund net cash flows (distributions minus contributions), yields a fund net present value equal to zero.

Both the TVPI and IRR performance measures have serious shortcomings. TVPI does not adjust for timing or for risk, and so cannot be used to directly compare performance across funds. The problems with IRR are well-known and described in any standard finance textbook, but they are particularly apparent in PE (see Phalippou, 2008, 2013). IRR's flaws derive from two sources. First, it is scale and horizon free, meaning it does not account properly for the value investors receive (or don't receive) from intermediate payments and time-in-investment. For example, would one rather receive a 100% return per year on one dollar over one year, or a 30% return per year on $100 million over 10 years? As IRR is often applied, it implicitly assumes that the LP could have reinvested their funds at the IRR.[10] Second, like TVPI, IRR does not adjust for risk, nor does it make a relative comparison to public market performance.

---

[8]Gompers *et al.* (2016) find, in a survey of 79 buyout GPs, that 38% of their LPs use TVPI as their main benchmark for performance evaluation, and 25% use IRR as their key performance metric. Gompers *et al.* (2020) report that of 546 institutional VCs, 63% use TVPI to evaluate investment opportunities, and 42% use IRR (many investors use both metrics, which is why the percentages sum up to over 100%).

[9]This same measure is sometimes referred to as multiple of invested capital, or MOIC.

[10]Modified IRR (MIRR) is sometimes used to address the reinvestment assumption, but it requires an additional assumption on the reinvestment rate to be used.

A third performance metric, Public Market Equivalent (PME) aims to address the weaknesses of TVPI and IRR. Originally developed in Long and Nickels (1996), it was redefined by Kaplan and Schoar (2005), whose version is sometimes referred to as KS-PME. The KS-PME has gained substantial popularity in recent years, and it is increasingly becoming a standard reporting metric.[11] At its heart, KS-PME is essentially a discounted TVPI that uses realized returns on a public benchmark (e.g., the S&P 500) as the discount rate. KS-PME divides the present value of distributions and the residual NAV by the present value of capital calls, with both present values taken from fund inception. The KS-PME answers the question "How much value has been distributed per $1 of present value invested?" A KS-PME of 1.18 means that one would have required starting with $1.18 in the relevant benchmark per $1 invested in PE to obtain the same cash flows.

A slightly different definition of PME, by Korteweg and Nagel (2016), computes the discounted value of net cash flows (distributions minus contributions, scaled by committed capital), as this has better econometric properties. The KN-PME is very close to the traditional concept of net present value, and addresses the question: "How much value has been added?" A KN-PME of zero means that no value was added relative to investing in the benchmark portfolio.

A final recent performance measure that has gained some traction, Direct Alpha, proposed by Gredil *et al.* (2014), is defined as the return that must be added to the benchmark to make KS-PME equal to one (or the KN-PME equal to zero). Gredil *et al.* (2014) explain that "...one can think of Direct Alpha as an annualized KS-PME taking into account both the performance of the reference benchmark and the precise times at which capital is actually employed". As such, Direct Alpha measures PE performance in a way that is more comparable to the alpha measure of performance used in standard asset pricing.

---

[11]Papers that report PMEs for various PE strategies include Kaplan and Schoar (2005); McKenzie and Janeway (2008); Phalippou and Gottschalg (2009); Higson and Stucke (2012); Axelson *et al.* (2013); Acharya *et al.* (2013); Harris *et al.* (2014a); Phalippou (2014); Fang *et al.* (2015); Robinson and Sensoy (2016); Braun *et al.* (2017); Harris *et al.* (2018); Phalippou (2020); Lerner *et al.* (2022); Andonov *et al.* (2020).

Sørensen and Jagannathan (2015) show that a PME can be interpreted as a present value calculation for an investor who has log-utility preferences, that is, whose stochastic discount factor (SDF) equals the reciprocal of the public market return. Following that result, Korteweg and Nagel (2016) specify a Generalized Public Market Equivalent (GPME) that allows for more flexible SDFs. Specifically, they assume a functional form to the SDF that corresponds to the valuation of a constant relative risk aversion (CRRA) investor, calibrated to price T-bills and equity returns. Thus, GPME answers the question "What net present value would a simple CRRA investor, calibrated to price public equity and riskless asset returns, give to the PE investment?" The GPME method includes PME as a special case but, as is usual with performance measurement, additional assumptions (in this case, pricing assets with a CRRA utility function) are used to generate clearer results, and the validity of the underlying functional form assumptions is difficult to test.

Finally, we note that the discount factor in the PME is the public stock market, which excludes private equity (as well as other asset classes). If the (G)PME is interpreted as simply benchmarking PE against the public equity market, then this is not an issue. However, when PMEs are interpreted as a value-added metric, one should remember that the SDF specification typically includes the return on an investor's entire wealth portfolio.

4.2.2   The Distribution of Fund Performance Measures

Table 2.1 reports descriptive statistics for TVPI, IRR, and PME, for the various segments within PE, treating any residual NAV from unliquidated investments as a pseudo-distribution that occurs at the end of the sample period (which is standard practice). Average TVPI ranges from 1.28 for infrastructure funds to 1.89 for VC funds. Medians are of similar magnitude, except that the highest number (1.61) is found for buyout funds. Infrastructure funds also have the lowest average and median fund IRR (9.59% and 8.78%), and buyout has the highest numbers (16.21% and 14.00%) in the sample. The average PME ranges from 0.86 for infrastructure to 1.11 for buyout, and the median varies between 0.86 (for natural resources) and 1.10 (for buyout).

Figure 4.1, Panels A and B, provide more detail by showing the kernel-smoothed distribution of TVPI and IRR, respectively. The most salient features are the (mostly positive) skewness and the heavy tails in most segments. Some of these non-normalities come from the time-series, as one can infer from the aggregate return statistics in Table 3.1. However, the lion's share of non-normalities arise in the cross-section, appearing strongly across funds raised in the same vintage year (results not shown).

An assumption behind MPT, as described in Section 3.1, is that investors either do not care about higher moments of returns, or that returns are jointly normally distributed so that all higher moments are zero. The latter assumption is clearly incorrect for PE. Kraus and Litzenberger (1976), Harvey and Siddique (2000), and Barberis and Huang (2008), amongst others, argue that investors should find the lottery-like feature of positive skewness attractive. This is especially true if there is a systematic component to the skewed payoffs (as captured by co-skewness with other assets). Thus, optimal weights on VC, which is strongly positive skewed, should be pushed up. At the same time, buyout and (especially) VC also exhibit large excess kurtosis relative to the Normal distribution, which could reduce optimal portfolio weights. But, maybe these distinctions don't matter? Levy and Markowitz (1979) and Kroll *et al.* (1984) argue that investors do almost as well (in expected utility terms) if they use mean-variance optimization instead of actual expected utility maximization, for a variety of utility functions, despite the presence of non-normalities. Thus:

Open Question 7: What is the impact of non-normalities in PE returns on optimal portfolio weights?
Most PE strategies have skewed returns with excess kurtosis relative to the Normal distribution. How do these non-normalities impact optimal PE portfolio weights? Is it important to perform actual expected utility maximization, or do mean-variance portfolio weights achieve a similar solution?

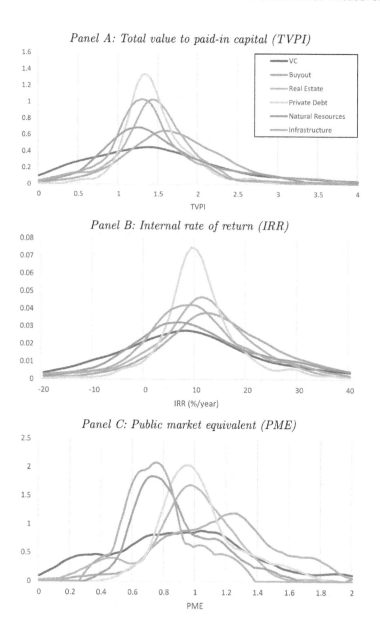

Figure 4.1: Distribution of private equity fund returns. Panel A shows the distribution of TVPI (total value to paid-in capital multiple) for private equity funds with a North American geographic focus and vintages from 1969 to 2014, by PE asset class. Funds of funds, secondary funds, co-investments, and venture debt funds are excluded. Panel B shows the distribution of the IRR (internal rate of return), and Panel C, the Kaplan and Schoar (2005) PME (public market equivalent) using the S&P 500 as the benchmark.

Applying the GPME to VC funds, Korteweg and Nagel (2016) find that performance is worse than PME suggests: the KN-PME is +0.05 but the GPME is −0.10 for the average VC fund in their sample. The GPME result suggests that investors would have been better off investing their money in a public stock market investment that is levered to have the same level of market risk as the average VC fund. Andonov *et al.* (2020) find that PE infrastructure and real estate funds also have negative GPME, as do Jeffers *et al.* (2021) for impact funds. Gredil *et al.* (2020b) expand the GPME to include factors from consumption-based asset pricing models: external habit formation and long-run risks. They find small net-of-fee outperformance for VC and insignificant results for BO. Gupta and Van Nieuwerburgh (2020) instead add bond market risks and other equity exposures such as real estate and infrastructure, and they estimate prices of strip securities, similar to Arrow-Debreu assets, instead of directly estimating the SDF. They find insignificant outperformance for VC, BO, real estate, and infrastructure PE funds.

4.2.3 Manipulating Performance Measures

Unfortunately, all performance measures are subject to manipulation. The most direct strategy is simply to manipulate NAVs. This is effective because it is common practice for active funds with unexited investments to include any residual NAV from unliquidated investments as a (pseudo) distribution in the calculation of TVPI, IRR, and (G)PME. This manipulation is particularly relevant because GPs raise follow-on funds while their initial fund is still in its intermediate stages (usually two to four years into the fund, when NAV is substantial and has a first-order impact on performance measures).

Summarizing the literature, Phalippou and Gottschalg (2009) show that NAVs are manipulated in the sense that investments are not written off when they should be and that they are reported selectively. Jenkinson *et al.* (2013) show that NAVs are generally low and smoothed (in line with conservativeness that gives rise to staleness in returns as discussed in the previous section), but that they are inflated during fundraising periods. Chakraborty and Ewens (2018) find that some VCs delay revealing negative information until after a new fund is raised. Barber and Yasuda

(2017) add that NAV inflation is concentrated in low-reputation GPs. Brown *et al.* (2019) also find that under-performing managers tend to overstate NAVs, but that these GPs are less likely to raise a follow-on fund, and they infer that LPs are able to see through the manipulation. They find that top-performing GPs appear to understate valuations. In contrast, Hüther (2021) looks at deal-level performance and does not find inflated performance. Instead, any manipulation occurs through the timing of deals rather than their valuation. He finds that buyout deals created shortly before fundraising under-perform similar to deals by non-fundraising firms. Finally, Jenkinson *et al.* (2020) find that NAV bias is worse in VC than in buyout.

A second way to manipulate performance measures is to change the timing of cash flows, since both investment and exit timing (i.e., capital calls and distributions) are fully under the GP's control. Unlike NAV manipulation, which is temporary by nature, cash flow timing strategies can make fund performance permanently appear higher, even for liquidated funds. IRR in particular is relatively easy for a GP to manipulate using timed capital calls and distributions (Phalippou, 2008, 2013) – for example, quick flip investments generate very high IRRs. Phalippou (2013) constructs an example that demonstrates how to use mediocre investment returns with moderate manipulation of investment timing to generate an apparently impressive IRR of 30% over a long time horizon. TVPI is not subject to such concerns, as it does not consider cash flow timing, which is why LPs often use it in conjunction with IRR. (G)PME is also less manipulable as it (implicitly) assumes that any reinvested distributions earn the benchmark rate of return, mitigating the reinvestment rate assumption baked into IRR (similar to the Modified IRR "fix"). We discuss the incentives and results around cash flow timing in more detail in Section 4.2.4.

A third and very direct way to manipulate performance is with leverage. Schillinger *et al.* (2019) and Albertus and Denes (2020) show that GPs often use subscription lines of credit (SLCs – lines of credit using LPs' committed capital as collateral) to create flexibility in capital call timing. This may be benevolent in the sense of reducing transactions costs by combining several small capital calls or preventing a deal from collapsing if LPs are slow to provide capital when called. However, some

GPs use SLCs more aggressively to delay capital calls, which makes it appear as if portfolio company returns were earned over a shorter time period. This increases the reported IRRs and PMEs. In addition, a GP's portfolio returns will exceed hurdle rates more often, leading to higher carried interest fees. Moreover, as demonstrated with the 2018 collapse of the Abraaj group, LPs may be held responsible for the loans, which are typically secured against committed capital, and they may thus be exposed to the credit risk of other LPs.[12]

Korteweg and Nagel (2016) show that GPME, unlike PME, properly reflects the impact of leverage on performance. For example, levering up a PE fund with an equal amount of debt doubles the expected GPME. This is not generally true for PME because the short bond position is discounted at the stock market rate of return.[13] This can be corrected if the degree of leverage is known. Given that leverage magnifies risk-adjusted returns, investors need to have a clear picture of the amount of credit used to properly evaluate managers' performance, but the extent and timing of credit line use is currently not generally disclosed to LPs.

Open Question 8: How easy is it for GPs to game standard performance measures, and does a manipulation-proof measure exist?
At present there is no theory that analyzes and compares the ease of gaming the standard PE performance measures (TVPI, IRR, (G)PME) through NAV inflation, cash flow timing, and leverage, and that shows how the fund fee structure affects GPs' incentives to engage in window dressing. Is there a manipulation-proof performance metric along the lines proposed by Goetzmann et al. (2007)? If not, what is the theoretical best that can be done?

---

[12]See, for example, https://www.economist.com/finance-and-economics/2019/05/18/the-biggest-collapse-in-private-equity-history-will-have-a-lasting-impact.

[13]Only if investors have log-utility preferences does PME correctly account for leverage, since PME uses the correct SDF in this special case (Sørensen and Jagannathan, 2015).

Returning to the issue of portfolio formation, a final problem is that the usual performance metrics do not fit the standard portfolio allocation setup:

Open Question 9: Is there a fund performance measure that can accommodate the standard portfolio allocation framework?

The common performance metrics (TVPI, IRR, (G)PME) do not naturally fit into the standard portfolio allocation setup, which presumes the availability of returns measured at regular intervals. Is there a way to incorporate them, or alternatively, is there a performance measure that is easily adaptable to the computation of optimal portfolio weights?

In summary, the current measures of private equity performance are unsatisfactory. That said, variations on the PME, like the GPME, are likely the best available. Those measures can be used to do a limited risk adjustment by choosing the appropriate benchmark, or by calibrating discount rates to CRRA investors. They are also less sensitive to timing manipulation than IRR. However, they do not fit well into the standard portfolio allocation framework.

Finally, missing prices may solve agency problems as well as cause them. It may be that part of the PE value proposition is to allow LPs to hide time-series volatility, enhancing manager entrenchment, enabling reaching for yield and other similar activities. The important agency problem may not be between the LP and the GP, but instead within the LP's organization or between the LP and its constituents or regulators. Cochrane (2021) writes that institutions may like PE assets "precisely because the assets are hard to mark to market, easy to just pay out 5% of a made-up value, not to sell in a panic, and not fire the asset manager based on an irrelevant price [for a long-term investor]". The idea that short-term performance measures may not be good guides for long-term investors is also discussed by David Swensen, the well-known former chief investment officer of the Yale endowment, in ProPublica (2009): "anointing winners and losers on the basis of 12 months' worth of performance is silly in the context of portfolios that are being managed with incredibly long time horizons". We don't know of any explicit documentation of the relative importance of the above effects:

Open Question 10: What is the most relevant agency problem?

Missing prices and manipulated NAVs may solve agency problems as well as cause them. How important is the agency problem within the LP (between the LP and its constituents or regulators) relative to the agency problem between the LP and GP? How does the absence of mark-to-market pricing play relate to these agency problems? Is it a bug or a feature from the LP's perspective?

4.2.4 Selected Entry and Exit

A simple model of PE goes as follows: a GP searches out potential portfolio companies to which they can add value, does deals when they become available, truthfully reports NAVs as the GP improves the portfolio companies' performance or growth options, and then sells the portfolio company in an IPO or merger and acquisition (M&A) transaction when the improvement is complete. Stated baldly, this model is clearly wrong – both entry and exit are selected – but something like it must be true if one takes IRRs and PMEs at face value, particularly for funds that are not yet fully liquidated.

Selected entry and exit presents a major problem in any type of performance evaluation, including fund returns, industry returns, and assessments of GP skill. Selection effects are especially important in deal-level data, where bankrupt portfolio companies are often not observed and there is no final settling up (unlike what happens at the fund level at liquidation). A further concern is that entry and exit selection is not idiosyncratic. Instead, both capital calls (capital entry into PE funds) and distributions (capital exit from PE funds) have systematic components (see, e.g., Harris *et al.*, 2014a; Robinson and Sensoy, 2016). We defer a more detailed discussion of systematic liquidity effects to Section 6, and focus here on the impact of selected entry and exit on assessing fund-level performance.

First, exit is clearly selected. As Cochrane (2005) observes with respect to VC, "the distribution of total (not annualized) returns is quite stable across horizons. This finding contrasts strongly with the typical pattern that the total return distribution shifts to the right and spreads out over time as returns compound. A stable total return is, however, a signature pattern of a selected sample. When the winners are pulled off the top of the return distribution each period, that distribution does not grow with time." The focus in Cochrane (2005) is on the risk and return of VC, and adjusting for selection effects drives down the estimated mean log return and drives up the estimated volatility. Korteweg and Sørensen (2010) confirm this finding in a later sample. Using an empirical methodology that allows for more covariates, they show that the selection effects on return and volatility, while weaker than in Cochrane (2005), remain of first-order importance.[14]

Robinson and Sensoy (2013) examine fee structures and show that some exit timing effects are consistent with agency problems between the GP and LP. As they describe (see also Choi *et al.*, 2013), after the preferred return to the LP has been cleared, the GP typically enters a catch-up period, during which they earn 100% of the net return on exits until it is as if they earned 20% on all previous investments (the waterfall). This creates an incentive for the GP to accelerate distributions immediately after the waterfall date, and, in fact, "distributions cluster around the 'waterfall' date". A second effect comes from a fee basis change: for many funds, the basis for management fees changes from invested capital to net invested capital (subtracting distributions) in years 4 or 5. In fact, "funds whose fee basis changes from committed capital to net invested capital are indeed more likely to exit investments later in the fund's life". Moreover, "times of high fundraising activity are associated with higher fixed management fees but are unrelated

---

[14]Ritter and Welch (2002) also highlight the endogeneity of exits through initial public offerings to market conditions: "If a bear market places too low a value on the firm, given the knowledge of entrepreneurs, then they will delay their IPOs until a bull market offers more favorable pricing". They "interpret the evidence on the going-public decision as suggesting that firms go public in response to favorable market conditions, but only if they are beyond a certain stage in their life cycle".

to carried interest or GP ownership terms. Thus, during fundraising booms, GP compensation rises and shifts to fixed components."

Barber and Yasuda (2017) report further evidence that GPs time distributions to coincide with fundraising, and that exit timing is managed in combination with NAV valuations. However, it is difficult to disentangle whether the GPs are changing the timing of fundraising, exits, or both. Brown *et al.* (2019) instead interpret the coincidence of distributions and fundraising as a form of costly signaling: early exits of high return investments signal that those profitable exits do exist in time to raise new funds, even though the exits may lower overall value. As such, the exit decision is not intended to make performance metrics appear better than they really are. Instead, this mechanism is somewhat similar to the grand-standing story in Gompers (1996), in which young VCs try to establish a reputation before fundraising, by pushing some portfolio companies to exit earlier than what may have been optimal to maximize returns. Hüther *et al.* (2020) claim that the timing of carried-interest payments specified in the LPA also affects exit timing. Specifically, compared to LP-friendly whole-fund contracts, "GP-friendly exit times more closely match the expected evolution of the underlying asset valuations of the portfolio companies in question". Moreover, if no distributions have yet been made to LPs, LP-friendly contracts "have longer waiting times to exit than deal-by-deal funds, consistent with the idea that the incentives to delay exits given whole-fund contracts are strongest in situations when the bulk of the realized return would be forfeited by the GP".

The previously mentioned studies generally assume that all portfolio companies are improved by GPs in qualitatively similar ways. However, this is not necessarily the case: for example, portfolio companies are both found and developed, and it may be that some companies are profitable investments because they are bought cheaply and some are profitable because they can be developed successfully. Sagi (2021) shows an analogous result in real estate returns: that there is an initial variance of returns due to mispricing or search frictions, and then additional variance as investments are held over time. Sørensen (2007) provides a model of VCs matching with portfolio companies while adding value in different ways. Any such heterogeneity would link selected exit and liquidity with underlying portfolio company characteristics and the GP's incentives. Because capital calls and distributions (entry and exit) are optimal choices by the GP, we can ask:

Open Question 11: How does the GP determine when specific portfolio companies will exit?

Cochrane (2005) provides an answer in an older sample of VC firms, and Korteweg and Sørensen (2010) follows with a different methodology on a more recent sample. However, neither study deals with BO or other types of PE, and both studies assume that variance grows constantly over time. Implicitly, this assumption means that GPs add value over time, instead of finding mispriced companies – companies they can flip for positive returns by alleviating the mispricing. The quantitative results may not generalize to BO because the search for mispriced firms is likely to be particularly relevant in buyout.

Do the Sagi (2021) variance decomposition results from real estate hold up in private equity data? This question is of wider interest to PE research because answering it would show how PE firms create value.

Open Question 12: How important is selected exit to LPs?

This is a follow-up to Open Question 11. In a baseline model in which all portfolio companies are the same and value creation is driven by geometric Brownian motions, entry and exit timing impacts the quantity of invested capital, but not its average return. How important are the deviations from this simple homogenous model to an LP?

4.3   General Partner Skill

The traditional measure of manager skill in the asset pricing literature is gross alpha (that is, risk-adjusted return before fees paid to the manager). Most papers that use individual investment-level data in PE (which is reported gross of fees) find strong evidence of alpha in both VC and buyout (e.g., Axelson *et al.*, 2014; Buchner and Stucke, 2014; Cochrane, 2005; Guo *et al.*, 2011; Korteweg and Sørensen, 2010). However, most of these studies report an alpha for the asset class, estimated on a large sample of investments, rather than GP-level alphas. Thus, while these results may be indicative of skill in the PE industry overall, they are not informative about *which* managers have skill, or if any manager can persistently outperform. If a GP truly has skill, then this should show up as persistence in risk-adjusted returns. Braun *et al.* (2017) report that in a large sample of buyout deals, a GP's previous deal's performance is a strong predictor of the next deal's return, even after controlling for GP experience, the age of the fund, leverage, and other factors. However, predictability has declined as the PE industry has matured. Acharya *et al.* (2013) find evidence of heterogeneous GP skills in buyouts by large, mature European PE firms. They show that GPs with operational backgrounds are able to generate portfolio company value through operational improvements, whereas those with a finance background are more successful following a mergers and acquisitions strategy. Biesinger *et al.* (2020) find that execution (more so than selection of strategies) is a key driver of outperformance in buyout.[15] There is also some evidence that GPs have some skill in timing exits when public stock market valuations are high: Gredil (2022) shows that high distributions generally predict lower future returns at the industry level, and that 50–70% of this result is due to GPs having superior information rather than them simply going with the cycle.

The bulk of the existing empirical evidence on PE performance persistence is based on fund-level data, which is easier to collect than individual investment-level data, but is reported net of fees. Although these results are more directly relevant for the LP's portfolio decision, this complicates inference regarding GP skill. The literature finds strong

---

[15] A large number of studies use non-return outcome measures to study whether PE firms create value, with mixed results (e.g., Agrawal and Tambe, 2016; Baker and Gompers, 2003; Bernstein and Sheen, 2016; Bernstein *et al.*, 2016; Bharath *et al.*, 2014; Boucly *et al.*, 2011; Chevalier, 1995; Cohn *et al.*, 2014, 2021a,b; Davis *et al.*, 2014; Eaton *et al.*, 2020; Ewens and Marx, 2018; Ewens *et al.*, 2022; Fracassi *et al.*, 2020; Gupta *et al.*, 2020; Leslie and Oyer, 2009; Lerner *et al.*, 2011; Nanda *et al.*, 2020; Spaenjers and Steiner, 2020; Sørensen, 2007). A detailed discussion of these papers falls outside of the scope of this monograph.

evidence of net-of-fee performance persistence in the PME of funds managed by the same GP.[16] Kaplan and Schoar (2005) use an autoregressive model to document that the performance of a GP's prior fund's return strongly correlates with the next fund's return. Robinson and Sensoy (2016) report that persistence has persisted in a longer time-series sample. Various studies introduce refinements to the Kaplan–Schoar approach. For example, Phalippou and Gottschalg (2009) correct for biases in reported interim net asset values (NAVs), yet still find strong persistence. Hochberg *et al.* (2014) show that adding the interim performance of the GP's most recent fund helps to predict performance of the next fund. Phalippou (2010) and Chung (2012), on the other hand, report that persistence is concentrated in poorly performing funds. Both papers also find weaker predictability when using the second-to-last fund return instead of the most recent fund, suggesting that persistence is short-lived, or that it is mechanically driven by the overlap between subsequent funds. Korteweg and Sørensen (2017) control for the overlap between funds and find that there is still evidence of long-horizon autocorrelation in returns, although it is difficult to capitalize on due to the noisiness in estimating GP skill. Li (2014) considers VC and buyout separately and finds stronger persistence in buyout. However, Harris *et al.* (2014b) look at predictability for buyout within subperiods and find that persistence has weakened after the turn of the millennium. To summarize the evidence, while the literature finds historical evidence of persistence, it is not clear whether this will still be true going forward.[17]

A small literature considers the impact of fund size on fund performance (e.g., Harris *et al.*, 2014a; Kaplan and Schoar, 2005; Lopez-de-Silanes *et al.*, 2015). On the one hand, buyout may be more scalable

---

[16]Note that the SDF approach (which includes the PME metric) yields a risk-adjusted performance metric while bypassing the estimation of factor loadings. In fact, SDF models and factor models are closely related: a linear SDF implies a linear factor model, and vice versa. One advantage of using SDFs over factor models is that they can be more flexible and are less sensitive to distributional assumptions (see Korteweg and Nagel, 2016). A few studies on performance persistence use IRRs or TVPIs, which do not consider risk, leaving open the possibility that persistence is driven by differences in risk-taking rather than skill.

[17]One might be concerned that staleness in NAVs causes persistence in returns, but the persistence literature uses mainly IRRs, TVPIs, and PMEs. For liquidated funds, NAVs do not enter these performance metrics, so this is not a primary concern.

than VC in the sense that the aggregate size of the asset class is considerably larger than VC (per Figure 2.1), as are individual fund sizes (see Table 2.1). On the other hand, Harris *et al.* (2014a) find suggestive evidence that larger VC funds have higher PMEs than smaller ones in the same vintage year, but there is little evidence that GP skill in buyout scales easily with fund size. Lopez-de-Silanes *et al.* (2015) also find no relationship between buyout fund size and returns, but they do find decreasing returns to scale when considering the number of simultaneous investments by a buyout GP. To a certain extent, the fact that a measure of skill is not easily scalable provides reassurance that the metric may indeed be capturing skill, rather than something that is easily replicable, like financial engineering.

The evidence of net-of-fee persistence requires an examination of the reasons why GPs do not take all the rents, for example by increasing fees or raising larger funds, as in Berk and Green (2004). There are several explanations that are based on LP pricing power that we discuss in Section 5: GPs may prefer a stable investor base to minimize the cost of raising new funds, LPs may have private information that they can use to hold up GPs, GPs may need to offer a premium to attract liquid LPs, or there may be search frictions in finding high quality GPs or LPs. One additional GP-centered explanation for net-of-fee performance persistence is the signalling model of Marquez *et al.* (2015). They assume that fees are set before investment opportunities are known to anyone. Once the opportunity set becomes known, GPs choose fund size and exert costly effort to signal their value-adding skill to entrepreneurs. The limitation on fund size is associated with excess returns for LPs.

Open Question 13: What is the source of performance persistence at the GP level?

In particular, what are the important channels? This question can be paired with a similar question about LP performance persistence (Open Question 14), but it is not clear that GP and LP performance persistence must be quantitatively driven by the same underlying channel(s). Are there additional GP-centered explanations?

5

Limited Partner Returns and Pricing Power

A core piece of the asset allocation problem for an LP is how to choose and manage relationships with individual GPs. Unlike a security such as common equity, a PE commitment or investment is not made at a single market price. There is a great deal of evidence that some LPs are able to extract higher returns from their investments than others, and they do so on a persistent basis. It appears that both GPs and LPs exhibit some pricing power. We begin by documenting these facts and reviewing some of the literature that supports the differential returns for LPs. Then we consider how these persistent return differences arise. We review several explanations, including variation in LP size and the ability to provide liquidity or exploit information. We close with a discussion of LP goals – some LPs have preferences over non-pecuniary characteristics of portfolio companies, such as location and social impact, that are attained at the cost of lower returns.

5.1   Persistent Return Differences

5.1.1   The Current State

There appear to be substantial and persistent differences in individual LP returns that are consistent with differences in skill. Cavagnaro *et al.* (2019) document that LP ability to pick successful GPs is persistent and exists across time periods in both BO and VC. A one-standard-deviation increase in skill is associated with a 1–2% increase in IRR. More, the results also hold for picking both first-time and reinvested funds, across which LP access would presumably vary. The authors conclude that, even above differences in access, "variation in skill is an important driver of institutional investors' returns".

As we detail, there is active work on what constitutes "skill" – what generates performance persistence – and how it can be broken down into recognizable pieces. LPs differ in how desirable they are to GPs, with the result that LPs have some pricing power and differential access to various investment vehicles. Not only do LPs experience return differentials by selecting different PE investments, there are also return differences between LPs in the same underlying fund. These return differences are consistent with increased access to desirable investments and with special breaks on fees. The evidence is consistent with performance persistence for LPs throughout the sample; however, the variation in types of PE investment have increased over time, with more clearly differentiated products and price discrimination later in the sample.

In recent work, Begenau and Siriwardane (2020) find that there is significant variation in net-of-fees performance in the same underlying fund. In comparing different public pension plans investing in the same GP fund, they show that some pension plans earn consistently higher net-of fees return (i.e., there is an LP-specific fixed effect). In addition, larger LPs (in terms of assets under management) with stronger ties to the GP (investment history) have better returns, and the effect is $6.8–$8.5 per $100 invested (dollar shortfall, un-discounted). The strong quasi-linear relationship between fund performance and the range of net-of-fees outcomes implies that the net-of-fees performance gap is due to carry rates that vary by 10–20% across investors in the same fund.

Recent work, including Fang *et al.* (2015), Braun *et al.* (2020), and Lerner *et al.* (2022), shows that the variation in PE vehicles has increased dramatically over time. LPs may now co-invest with GPs under different fee structures and deal choices than the GP's main fund. Braun *et al.* (2020) find that co-investments, on a gross-of-fees basis, are comparable to the GP's main fund, but that, net-of-fees, co-investments outperform fund investments by a significant margin. Using a different sample, Lerner *et al.* (2022) find that co-investments, on a net-of-fees basis, match the broader PE market but lag the GP's main fund. Both papers note that experience in previous co-investments is a determinant of returns, and they both agree that the evidence does not favor an adverse selection story in which GPs offer bad investments outside their main fund.

Lerner *et al.* (2022) present evidence of an interaction effect in past performance between LPs and GPs. Their sample is the set of asset owners for which State Street acts as a custodian, and the interaction effect is concentrated in discretionary vehicles (in which LPs can determine which deals are included) rather than GP-directed vehicles. Matches between high-past-performance LPs and similar GPs are associated with returns that are better than their respective histories would indicate on their own. Similarly, matches between low-past-performance GPs and LPs under-perform. Their results "support the idea that top GPs take into consideration the outside options of their LPs when offering them access to [alternative vehicles]", and that "the identity of the LP has become more important in the investment process".

5.1.2 Maturation of the Industry

In the early and less developed phase of PE, there were large, persistent differences in returns across LP types (endowments, pensions, etc.), but those differences have become much smaller. In fact, the returns to skill seem to have declined over time both within and among LP-types.[1]

---

[1]The analogous result for GPs, from Harris *et al.* (2014b), is that performance persistence among buyout funds was strong prior to 2000 and nonexistent afterwards. In contrast, performance persistence among VC GPs was high before 2000 and has remained high.

In the earlier period (before the tech bubble collapse in 2000), Lerner *et al.* (2007) document that endowments notably outperformed other LP types, partly because of better investment choices (e.g., less home bias) or better access, but mostly through an unobserved persistent factor related to LP type. In contrast, Cavagnaro *et al.* (2019) and Sensoy *et al.* (2014) find that while there are persistent return differences across LPs, there are no persistent return differences across LP types in the later period (2000–2011). More generally, the returns to skill have declined over time even within types. Further, Sensoy *et al.* (2014) disagree on the relative importance of access, observing "the superior performance of endowment investors in the 1991–1998 period . . . is mostly due to their greater access to the top-performing venture capital partnerships. In the subsequent 1999–2006 period, endowments no longer outperform, no longer have greater access to funds that are likely to restrict access, and do not make better investment selections than other types of institutional investors." Sensoy *et al.* (2014) and Cavagnaro *et al.* (2019) attribute the overall changes to the maturing of the PE industry.

5.2 Specific Explanations for Access and Pricing Power

Access to GPs is limited, and this is particularly true for successful GPs, whose funds are typically over-subscribed. In fact, the existence of different types of vehicles offered to different LPs (see Sections 2.4 and 5.1) is clear evidence of differences in access. But, what are the specific things that GPs and LPs value that either require or allow for differential access?[2]

As we show, there appears to be substantial variation in the desirability of LPs, and that this variation is linked to pricing power by LPs, returns to scale in due diligence for LPs, and price discrimination by GPs. Research into the specific features of LPs that are desirable include funding stability, size, and past match-specific experience (e.g.,

---

[2]This section also provides a partial answer to the question "How does the logic of Berk and Green (2004) work in the PE market?" In addition to the papers we outline below, Fulghieri and Sevilir (2009), Inderst *et al.* (2006), Kanniainen and Keuschnigg (2003), and Bernile *et al.* (2007) provide theories that explain why GPs, particularly in VC, might choose to limit their fund sizes.

information). This research has concluded that GPs respond with a fund design that includes variation in liquidity and deal quality to induce matches with the desired LPs.

5.2.1 Liquidity Provision, Information, and Search

Lerner and Schoar (2004) introduce the theory of funding insurance (liquidity provision) from LPs. Existing LPs know more about whether the source of existing fund returns is skill or luck, so GPs face a lemons problem when raising follow-on funds. However, some LPs have a propensity for liquidity shocks, and so may not be able to invest in follow-on funds even if performance is a result of skill. To avoid the lemons problem as much as possible, all GPs prefer existing LPs that can offer funding in all states of the world, i.e., LPs that can offer funding liquidity to GPs are more desirable. Since skilled GPs value those LPs more, they will engage in screening techniques, offering products with different liquidity provisions at different prices. Lerner and Schoar (2004) document results consistent with the theory, including a high degree of continuity in the investors of successful funds and suggestive evidence that investors can partially anticipate the returns of following funds.

Maurin et al. (2020) use a moral hazard model to explain fund structure and how it provides liquidity to LPs and GPs, and their model produces performance persistence as a consequence. LPs face exogenous funding liquidity shocks, and GPs face moral hazard in how investments are managed. The fund structure solves the optimal incentive problem. Capital is raised once and invested in multiple projects to make returns more informative: as in Laux (2001), seeing two separate positive outcomes is more informative about effort than seeing mixed outcomes. When a GP faces LPs with high liquidity needs, the GP calls more capital early, allowing them to withhold more if the LPs do not meet the second capital call. This has negative real effects, so GPs prefer more liquid LPs and offer a return premium.[3]

---

[3]One consequence of this model is that a more liquid secondary market is linked with lower persistence in GP returns, which is consistent with the gradual weakening of persistence in returns in buyout if not VC.

Hochberg *et al.* (2014) demonstrate match-specific pricing power by LPs. They apply an informational hold-up intuition to the fees and returns of follow-on funds. Existing LPs have soft information about whether the source of existing fund returns is skill or luck. They can threaten not to participate in a new fundraising by the GP, which would leave the GP to raise funds from outside LPs, who lack information and would draw negative inferences about the GP's quality knowing that the informed LPs are not committing to the new fund. To avoid the larger discount required to raise funds from outside LPs, GPs are willing to grant rents to informed LPs. The result is that LPs generate match-specific pricing power over time and use it to require GPs to offer better terms (lower fees or different investment features), leading to performance persistence over time.[4] Hochberg *et al.* (2014) document results, including on fundraising and pricing, that are consistent with the theory.

There are also several papers that posit search frictions to explain LP pricing power. Korteweg and Sørensen (2017) show that, because of the level of noise and idiosyncratic risk in PE performance, it is very hard to statistically identify high-quality GPs (see Sections 4.3 and 6.1 for more discussion). Thus, an LP that was able to identify good GPs would have an informational advantage in searching for new managers. Gârleanu and Pedersen (2018) explain how search and informational frictions can lead to performance persistence in the context of liquid equities.

Open Question 14: What are the sources of persistent LP return differentials?

What is the relative importance of the various proposed sources of persistence in LP performance? Persistence might represent the repeated use of resources and position, or just the pure ability to recognize good managers. How persistent are liquidity provision and

---

[4]Glode and Green (2011) also uses an information spillover story to explain performance persistence and other facts in hedge fund returns. However, their mechanism is very different from Hochberg *et al.* (2014) and would, if applied to PE, rely on the ability of outside GPs/LPs to successfully copy a trade. This assumption is less suitable to the PE industry.

informational advantages? More generally, which of these explanations is quantitatively more important? This question is of wider impact. Can we use PE to partially decompose or micro-found the black box of "skill" into observable pieces and resources?

Open Question 15: What model explains the formation of GP–LP matches?
There are several outstanding theories of why GPs might prefer certain types of LPs, and how both sides have some form of pricing power. How is that pricing power actually achieved, and how do GP-LP matches form? Gârleanu and Pedersen (2018) describe a search model for asset managers in the context of the asset-market structure of Grossman and Stiglitz (1980). Does their model generalize to the PE industry structure? Would an over-the-counter (OTC/)search-style model with persistent contacts provide insight?

5.2.2 Size

There is evidence that larger LPs may have superior ability to choose investments and obtain better terms overall. This is in addition to the direct effect of minimum capital commitments, which imply that large LPs are better able to diversify their holdings.

Dyck and Pomorski (2015) report, in a sample of defined benefit pension funds, that LPs with larger PE holdings obtain substantially better returns than LPs with smaller holdings. Part of the effect comes from size generating access to better intermediation – avoiding funds of funds, more no-fee co-investments – but the majority comes from superior gross returns, in excess of what proxies for access and experience would predict.[5] These results contrast with the results for GPs, especially in VC. For example, both Lopez-de-Silanes *et al.* (2015) and Metrick and Yasuda (2010) argue that there are diseconomies of scale in fund size. See Section 4.3 for further discussion of GP size.

---

[5]In contrast, Lerner *et al.* (2007) show negative but statistically insignificant effects of LP size on performance while Andonov *et al.* (2018) show results that are usually positive and sometimes statistically significant, but both of these results are limited and well outside the main questions that these papers address.

The LP outcomes from Dyck and Pomorski (2015) match with survey evidence from Da Rin and Phalippou (2017) on investment terms and due diligence. The authors look at the internal practices of LPs and find "The only consistently significant dimension along which LPs differ in their practices is the size of the private equity portfolio (in absolute value). The institutions with large allocations to private equity are those spending most time on due diligence for each fund and those undertaking the most initiatives in the due diligence process." Similarly, they show 63% of large LPs always get side letters, which allow for investment with terms that differ from a fund's standard terms (although the survey does not cover the specific content of the side letters). In contrast, only 17% of small LPs always obtain side letters. In addition, for older and larger partnerships, management fees for the GP may be negotiated every year rather than being set in advance. In an anecdotal way, Lee (2015) describes the contents of side letters, including differing fee structures and economic terms, most-favored nation (MFN) clauses, Freedom of Information Act (FOIA) aversion/avoidance behavior, and varying compliance needs.

In addition, minimum commitment requirements from LPs are standard (as described in Section 2), so it is mechanically true that larger LPs will have more opportunities to invest. It may also be that larger (and more experienced) LPs are simply better at understanding PE contracts and their somewhat opaque fee structures. But more than that, Braun *et al.* (2020) present evidence consistent with price discrimination based on size. In their broad sample, they note that co-investment opportunities offer significantly lower costs and fees from the GP's main fund. Moreover, these co-investments seem to be used to allow for larger deals that would be otherwise prohibitive for a given GP. Thus, co-investments may serve as a way to share the gains from expanding a GP's investment opportunity set.

Open Question 16: What is the relationship between LP size and returns?

In particular, how is it mediated? Minimum commitment require-
ments and the ability to conduct due diligence generate returns

to scale and directly affect contract terms and the ability to pick desirable GPs. However, it also seems possible that size could be a proxy for the ability to provide liquidity, and more investments would give an LP access to more information, both of which can separately lead to better returns and access. In addition, causality may run at least partially the other way: if an investor earns higher returns, they shift their portfolio and attract other funds to invest more in PE, thereby becoming a larger LP.

This question is also relevant for the wider intermediation literature. What is the relationship between an asset manager's (LP's) portfolio of illiquid assets and returns? How does it relate to the optimal size of the intermediary (GP)?

5.3   Differing Goals

A priori, it is clear that any goal other than financial returns will result in lower financial returns. The empirical question is how one can observe non-financial goals, and how much has to be given up to obtain them. It appears that non-financial goals are widespread, particularly in public institutions, and that the "how much" can be up to an IRR difference of about 5% on targeted investments.[6] That said, the aggregate loss in returns from non-financial goals is the product of the loss per investment and the fraction of the portfolio that is engaged, and this latter number is typically much less than one.[7]

---

[6] Aside from targeted investments, some VCs can act as strategic investors, consistent with the theories like Hellmann (2002) and Mathews (2006). For example, Hellmann *et al.* (2007) find that bank-affiliated VCs allow banks to build relationships and reduce information asymmetry with start-up companies. Similarly, Ma (2019) shows that corporate VC investments are often strategic with the goal of regaining their innovative edge after adverse shocks. However, these vehicles frequently combine the roles of LP and GP and a more detailed analysis is beyond the scope of the current survey.

[7] The results throughout this section appear to conflict with the results of Cavagnaro *et al.* (2019) mentioned earlier. The most likely explanation may be the role of noise in the differing econometric frameworks: the aggregate return differences due to goals is small relative to noise in returns and to other variation in skill.

Hochberg and Rauh (2012) and Andonov *et al.* (2018) examine the goals and returns of public pension funds. Hochberg and Rauh (2012) begin by detailing three stylized facts. First "institutional investors of all types exhibit substantial home bias in their PE portfolios", over-weighting in-state investments by 8.2% in aggregate. Second, in-state investments experience returns (IRRs) that are lower by 2–4%. Finally, pension funds exhibit more in-state bias (9.8% in aggregate) than other institutional investors, and cross-sectional differences are related to measures of state-level political self-dealing. The result is that public pensions under-perform. Andonov *et al.* (2018) broaden the findings. They observe that while inexperienced pension board members are associated with worse performance, pension fund under-performance is much more strongly related to the presence of political appointees (as opposed to members of the public or other backgrounds), and these political appointees have backgrounds that indicate that they are financially sophisticated. Further, the authors show (in the online appendix) that Economically Targeted Investments (ETIs), as a separate investment activity, have lower realized IRRs by 4–6%, but this does not explain the performance of political appointees. Instead, contributions and the need for political support (as defined in the paper) have more explanatory power. Taken together, these papers are strong evidence that public pensions are willing to trade off pension fund returns with both in-state investments/economic benefits (e.g., through ETIs) and apparent agency and political rents.

In a similar vein, Andonov *et al.* (2020) show that public institutions under-perform private institutions when investing in infrastructure deals, by about 1%. The deals themselves have similar observable characteristics, and, while local bias and related under-performance exist for both public and private investors, they do not explain the public–private gap. Instead, the authors conclude that their findings are consistent with public institutions exhibiting lower skill or having non-financial objectives.

Barber *et al.* (2021) find that investors sacrifice returns to invest in dual-objective (social impact) VC funds. The different goal is worth 4.6% in IRR, and "Investors with mission objectives and/or facing political pressure exhibit high WTP (willingness to pay); those subject to legal restrictions (e.g., ERISA) exhibit low WTP." Interestingly, GPs of impact funds do not have direct financial incentives to achieve the non-financial goals: Geczy *et al.* (2021) report that other contract provisions, such as governance, are instead adjusted to achieve these objectives.

6

Diversification and Liquidity

A fundamental part of the LP's asset allocation problem is how to build private equity portfolios out of investments in particular funds. How should the LP diversify across funds and co-investment opportunities? How should the LP manage their investments over time?

There are two important problems that LPs must overcome in order to diversify their investments. The first is that useful diversification requires large amounts of capital, which an LP may not have. Not only do GPs generally require minimum capital commitments, but PE funds have strong life-cycle cash flow effects: there is often a multi-year delay between an LP's capital commitment and capital call, and then a multi-year, illiquid investment. Doing a back-of-the-envelope calculation, a typical LP might achieve partial diversification by investing in three funds a year; with a minimum capital commitment of $5 million per fund, an average commitment period of three years, and an average holding period of five years, that LP would maintain a $120 million allocation to PE, with $75 million invested and $45 million additionally committed.[1]

The second problem is that portfolio diversification requires diversification across both return shocks and across timing shocks. Because private equity is a delegated investment, the GP retains discretion over the timing of calls and distributions, which means that once capital is committed, the GP retains control over the quantity that an LP has invested at any given time. LPs may be able to time their capital commitments, but that does not imply that they can successfully time when their capital is invested or when it exits. Diversifying across investments within a given time frame is different and easier than diversifying across time frames. Empirically, both call and distribution timing contain systematic components,[2] and high aggregate investment is followed by low aggregate performance.

This section addresses the question of how an LP, perhaps with limited capital, can effectively diversify their PE portfolio to account for PE's particular mix of idiosyncratic and systematic shocks.

6.1 Diversifying Cash Flows

The first observation is that there is a great deal of idiosyncratic risk in the timing and quantity of cash flows, so there ought be large gains from diversification across funds. This contrasts with the next set of results, which shows that diversification is in fact very difficult.

Robinson and Sensoy (2016) find that "most variation in fund-level cash flows is purely idiosyncratic across funds of a given age at a given point in time, or associated with life-cycle effects whereby funds call capital when they are young and distribute it as they age". By their

---

[1]For partial diversification from investing in three funds per year, see Gredil *et al.* (2020a). A $5 million minimum capital commitment is typical, as per DeLuce (2020) and Preqin (2016). Average commitment periods and investment periods vary between VC and BO, across periods, and across data sets; three years and five years are approximations of the results in Harris *et al.* (2014a) and Gourier *et al.* (2021). The capital requirement problem can be partially but not completely overcome by investing in funds of funds, as discussed below.

[2]See, additionally, Section 4.2 for a discussion of how selected timing happens on the individual fund level and its impact on performance measurement and evaluation.

calculations, the standard deviation of quarterly net cash flows for an average fund is 11.57% of committed capital for BO and 11.99% in VC, and those drop to 4.54% in BO and 4.09% in VC with full vintage-year diversification. Similarly, Korteweg and Sørensen (2017) show in a different sample and with different methods that most PE returns are idiosyncratic, so there should be substantial gains to diversification.

Idiosyncratic risk seems to generate a return premium for LPs; in a fully liquid market, a diversified investor would be able to capture that premium without taking the risk. Ewens *et al.* (2013) use a principal–agent model to show that idiosyncratic risk, not just systematic risk, will be compensated with additional alpha, even in competitive capital markets. The key insight is that general partners must put a significant fraction of their wealth into their funds, and the compensation for this risk is determined in contracts that are signed before investments are found. Thus the contracts can only compensate for the expected risk of portfolio companies, not the risk of the realized deals. In making each deal, the GP will be using their personal risk–return trade-off, not the one implied by the capital markets, and they will require a discount to invest in high-total-risk businesses. This discount is partially captured by GPs and partially by LPs, meaning that after-fee fund payouts will reflect total and idiosyncratic risk, not just capital market risk factors. Ewens *et al.* (2013) present cross-sectional empirical results consistent with this argument.

In addition, because PE payoffs are so skewed, diversification does more than simple risk reduction for welfare. Braun *et al.* (2020) observe that portfolios of about 10 (co-investment) buyout deals are needed for the median return to be greater than that of the median fund return. This result is driven by the very high skewness of portfolio company returns. Brown *et al.* (2020b) conduct a simulation exercise using historical returns and find that portfolios with an allocation to randomly selected private equity funds, in combination with public equity and bonds, on average outperformed portfolios with public equities and bonds alone (in terms of higher returns and less risk).

In recent work, Gredil *et al.* (2020a) quantify the importance of imperfect diversification for LPs using a method of moments framework and a welfare analysis. They report that if an LP invested 30% of their portfolio in PE and picked one fund per year, their certainty equivalent PME would be 4.9% lower (BO) or 7.5% lower (VC) than if they were able to obtain the vintage average for certain. A typical LP picks three funds per year, which results in a certainty equivalent PME that is 1.9% (BO) or 3.6% (VC) lower than for the vintage average.

Additional support for the value of risk-reduction through diversification comes from funds of funds (FoFs). Harris *et al.* (2018) analyze the returns of BO and VC FoFs. As one expects, FoFs offer significantly safer investments relative to direct funds, reducing the standard deviation of PMEs from 1.78 to 0.57 in VC and from 0.55 to 0.24 in BO. More, FoFs reduce the gap between mean and median PMEs (due to skewness), particularly for VC. That said, when comparing FoFs to portfolios of PE funds, they find "significantly lower returns [after fees] for FoFs that focus on buyouts or are generalist funds compared with portfolios formed by 'random' direct fund investing in similar direct funds. In contrast, FoFs in VC perform roughly on a par with portfolios of direct funds." Even so, reducing VC PME standard deviation by about a third with rough parity in the mean is a significant welfare improvement, and may be particularly attractive to smaller LPs that cannot diversify across many individual fund investments.

6.2   Diversifying with Hot and Cold Markets

The difficulty with diversification in PE is the presence of systematic liquidity shocks. In fact, given GP discretion over timing, diversifying cash flows might act to concentrate liquidity effects.

The aggregate level of PE investment varies dramatically from hot to cold periods, and periods with large quantities invested are followed by periods with low performance. In an early period sample, Gompers and Lerner (2000) document that capital inflows impact portfolio company valuations and give the first evidence of systematic liquidity effects in VC. Harris *et al.* (2014a) find that for buyout, as "capital commitments increase from the bottom quartile of years (0.42%) to the top quartile of years (0.87%), IRRs decline by more than 5% per year", while for VC, "when capital flows move from the bottom to top quartile, IRRs decline by 9% per year". Similarly, Robinson and Sensoy (2016) show that both capital calls and distributions are pro-cyclical in the sense that the market price–dividend ratio and the (negative) Baa–Aaa yield spread predict more calls and distributions. Distributions are more cyclical than calls, implying pro-cyclical aggregate cash flows to investors. Consistent with the notion of a liquidity premium, funds with less cyclical (or, more counter-cyclical) capital calls perform better.

These facts imply that LPs are more likely to have their capital called exactly when investment opportunities are worse. But, investors can control the timing of their commitments; is this enough for diversification over time? A key feature of the liquidity risk of PE is that the timing of calls and distributions is at the discretion of the GP. Brown *et al.* (2021) evaluate the gains from diversification across time and find "modest gains, at best, to pursuing realistic, investable strategies that time capital commitments to private equity". Using fundraising as a measure of cycles, the authors find for buyout "cash calls cluster over time even for the negatively correlated commitments made by pro-cyclical and counter-cyclical allocation strategies ... the correlation of distributions between pro-cyclical and counter-cyclical strategies is 0.81, even though the commitments are negatively correlated". Similar results are found for VC.

Private equity as a whole has significant exposure to systematic liquidity shocks that also affect public equity. Franzoni *et al.* (2012) find that "private equity suffers from significant exposure to the same liquidity risk factor as public equity and other alternative asset classes. The unconditional liquidity risk premium is close to 3% annually and, in a four-factor model, the inclusion of this liquidity risk premium reduces alpha to zero." The authors find support for a funding liquidity mechanism: "returns are significantly related to the tightening of credit standards. A one-standard-deviation increase in this measure of the deterioration in funding liquidity decreases the annual return by 15.9%. Second, when including both the measure of funding liquidity and that of market liquidity, we observe that funding liquidity absorbs half of the market liquidity effect."[3]

In addition, Peters (2018) finds that VC investments load positively on aggregate idiosyncratic volatility, and this is true at the portfolio company, fund, and asset-class levels. However, since the price of idiosyncratic volatility is negative, this result implies that the exposure to aggregate idiosyncratic volatility lowers VC returns. The loading and the price of risk result from a real-options intuition that fits the staged-VC environment better than the BO environment. The difference between Ewens *et al.* (2013) and Peters (2018) is that the former documents a positive cross-sectional relationship between idiosyncratic risk and returns, while the latter documents a negative time series relationship between aggregate idiosyncratic risk and returns.

6.3   The Secondary Market

One way out of the liquidity problem for LPs is to try to sell their stake on the secondary market. That market has developed rapidly in recent years, but is still not fully liquid. Nadauld *et al.* (2019) show that secondary market transactions occur at a 13.8% average discount to NAV (but remember that NAV is self-reported). More, in the secondary market buyers outperform sellers ex post using matched cash flow data. Attributing returns from fund inception through the secondary market sale to sellers and from the secondary market sale through termination to buyers, the authors compute annualized PMEs to show that return differences are about 2.7% per year for funds that are four to nine years old. Consistent with a liquidity story, discounts are larger when the (public) market-wide price/earnings ratio is low, for smaller transactions and for smaller and younger funds.

The structure of the secondary market, and who trades with whom, is not yet well understood. In recent research, Albuquerque *et al.* (2018)

---

[3] As a result, private equity does not appear to offer much benefit in diversifying away from liquidity shocks in public markets. At the same time, there may be a separate liquidity premium in PE that is not well picked up by the Pastor and Stambaugh (2003) factor, which measures liquidity most directly relevant in market microstructure.

fill in some of the gaps by fitting a structural/empirical model of the arrival of bids for LP stakes in the secondary market and test their model with broker data outside the financial crisis. Their results are more consistent with discounts for funding liquidity rather than for adverse selection or hidden information (except for small funds). Moreover, while secondary market funds are responsible for three-quarters of the bids in the paper's sample, liquidity (meaning buy offers after negative market liquidity shocks) is provided by LPs who do *not* specialize in secondary market acquisitions.

While Albuquerque *et al.* (2018) and Nadauld *et al.* (2019) examine transactions between LPs, Degeorge *et al.* (2016) examine transactions between GPs in which portfolio companies are transferred from one GP to another. The authors find that these transactions can be subject to agency problems, particularly if the buyer has money to burn or the buyer has a compensation agreement that grants fees that depend on capital invested. In contrast, transactions between GPs with complementarity skill sets are on average value adding. Can the LP–LP and GP–GP markets be jointly understood?

Open Question 17: How are the secondary market for LP stakes and the market for GP-to-GP sales of portfolio companies linked?

The secondary market for LP stakes seems to resemble an OTC market for large, otherwise illiquid investments. In addition, there is a simultaneous market for trading underlying portfolio companies from GP to GP. How are they linked empirically? Is there a theory that describes these markets jointly?

6.4 Diversification Trade-Offs

How do the benefits and difficulties of diversification trade off? If diversification within vintages is easy and diversification across vintages is unproductive, perhaps an optimal strategy is to simply have a target allocation that is relatively time-invariant. However, such a rule of thumb can result in bad outcomes in a dynamic world, especially in the face of the liquidity issues that plague PE. For example, when a public market crash occurs, LPs can find themselves above their PE target (the "denominator effect", possibly exacerbated by the stale price problem described above) and forced to liquidate PE fund commitments at fire-sale prices. It may be optimal to have a higher PE allocation in these periods and to fund any incoming capital calls out of other liquid assets.

Open Question 18: What are the (unintended) consequences of simple rule-of-thumb PE allocations?

There is a simple PE investment strategy: assign an allocation, build up commitments over time until that allocation is reached, and fund new commitments out of old commitments. How (sub)optimal is this strategy? Answering this question would follow and deepen the work started in Brown et al. (2021), in particular, the result that GP investment discretion makes pro-cyclical and counter-cyclical allocation strategies much less effective.

Anecdotal evidence suggests that the PE investment strategy above is common among some types of institutional investors.[4] Is this actually true when a broad sample of LPs is included? Maybe there is a simple cost argument, and larger LPs are actually much more diversified than smaller ones? Three funds a year seems insufficiently diversified, but perhaps it is unnecessary to commit capital every single year since GP discretion washes out most of the variation in commitment timing? More generally, knowing how LPs diversify their investments in practice and the associated cash flow outcomes would give portfolio theory a testable prediction or a target:

Open Question 19: How do LPs diversify their investments?

Answering this question would provide insight into what risks LPs are willing to tolerate and what risks require compensation. It would

---

[4]For example, pension funds and endowments often publish a slow-moving target allocation.

*shed light on a particularly relevant type of delegated portfolio –
the GP–LP interaction. In addition, are there PE-specific agency
problems inside LPs that induce inefficient diversification?*

An additional gain from diversification, learning through experience
and experimentation, is suggested by the results of Korteweg and
Sørensen (2017). The authors show that performance is persistent from
a variance decomposition, but there is so much noise that it is very
hard to figure out which firms in particular are high skill. Learning
about GPs is likely enhanced by investing in them, as opposed to simply
gathering publicly available information. One would need to diversify
across firm-years and fund-years to isolate the high-skill firms. Is there
an experiential value from doing so?

**Open Question 20: What is the value to LPs of experi-
menting with different GPs?**
*Data on private equity returns is incomplete (see, e.g., Harris et al.,
2014a for a partial discussion of the differences between several standard, but incomplete, data sets). Investing as an LP might make it
easier to identify good managers because of access to both additional
hard data from the relationship and soft information from interac-
tions with GPs. Also, what is the role for PE advisors/consultants
in this process?*

*This is both a theoretical and empirical question with wider
appeal: what is the value of experimenting with intermediaries in
markets with soft information?*

Finally, how do any empirical results on LP portfolio construction
compare to the results of different modelling frameworks? In particular,
is the observed diversification strategy more consistent with an optimal
investment policy or with an agency model that limits flexibility? Agency
problems between the GP and LP? Agency problems inside the LP?[5]

---

[5]Examples of agency problems inside an LP in a portfolio choice context include
models like Van Binsbergen *et al.* (2008) and Sharpe (1981).

Open Question 21: How do models of diversification and agency compare?

Agency and corporate finance models of investment emphasize very different frictions from models in the asset pricing and portfolio choice literature. What are the relative size of the frictions? Can model comparison be used to assess the size of the agency and relationship problems for the LP? How important are continued relationships relative to the expected returns on the immediate investment?

This question is related to Open Question 10: it may be that the private equity model is successful because it solves one set of agency problems at the cost of a different, lesser set of problems.

6.5   Buyout Booms and Busts

Because LPs have to agree to fund the quantity of investments made by GPs, cycles and waves of activity are not just economy-wide buying activity, they are also a pattern of commitments made by LPs and investments made by GPs. This fact gives us another way to examine the decision making of LPs: instead of examining the LP's investment problem at the individual or portfolio levels, we can use the aggregate level. And, not surprisingly, aggregate buyout activity responds to aggregate credit and equity market conditions.

This section focuses on buyout because there are many more results and the data is much more readily available than for VC (however, see Janeway *et al.*, 2021 for a review of VC cycles). In addition, we limit our analysis to buyout, avoiding a review of the entire M&A literature, which is well beyond the scope of this monograph.

The remainder of this section is written as if the M&A market were segmented into sub-markets for private equity (financial bidders) and strategic acquisition (corporate bidders) and deals only with financial bidders. In truth, the market is only partially segmented. A result that is helpful in establishing the existence of some segmentation comes from Gorbenko and Malenko (2014). They find that "different targets appeal to different types of bidders", and so the switch from strategic bidders to financial bidders is also associated with a switch in targets.

Implicitly, the two types of bidders might not be in direct competition in finding targets. More, "variation in valuations of financial bidders is captured to a large extent by observable target and economy-wide characteristics", like debt and equity market conditions, which is not true of strategic bidders. Their results are "consistent with different financial bidders applying similar post-acquisition strategies and each strategic bidder having relatively unique synergies. This finding suggests that different financial bidders appear to be more interchangeable than strategic bidders from the target's point of view." In other words, we can hope to consider financial and strategic M&A markets somewhat separately.

The difficulty with examining GP investments to determine LP decision making is that the two decisions are separate in time. This separation implies that GPs and LPs are making their individual investment decisions in response to different aggregate conditions. A preliminary step is to establish the extent to which GP investment timing is predictable given LP commitments. We can think of two complementary questions that have not been answered, to our knowledge:

Open Question 22: How predictable is aggregate financial-buyer acquisition activity from LP commitments made years earlier?

How responsive are GPs to aggregate conditions in choosing individual deals after LP commitments have been made? Brown et al. (2021) demonstrate that GPs have enough discretion to prevent LPs from effectively diversifying across time. However, while the link between LP commitments and GP investments is flexible in the short run, it is much more rigid over periods of four to six years simply because of the length of a fund's life. More, much of the short-term flexibility will be exhausted by the fact that the GP cannot find good opportunities at will.

Open Question 23: How elastic are the intensive and extensive margins for LP participation?

The restrictions on LP investment (e.g., access, minimum commitment, due diligence costs; see Section 5) imply that investors cannot move freely into private equity. Yet it is reasonable to think that new and existing investors in PE might behave differently – after all, they have already made different choices about past participation. What fraction of the changes in aggregate private equity holdings are driven by changes in the composition of LPs, and how much is driven by changes in portfolio allocation for existing LPs? Has this changed as the industry has matured and secondary markets have become more liquid? Is there a persistent relationship across the buyout booms and busts?

6.5.1   Equity Markets versus Debt Markets: Empirical Work

There is dispute as to whether credit market conditions or equity market conditions are more important to buyout activity. Importantly, the relative importance of debt and equity markets appears different when examining buyout timing and buyout financing composition. This distinction is important to LPs because it controls their opportunity set: given that GPs control investment timing, what market conditions will an LP actually realize for their investment?

Axelson *et al.* (2013) investigate the amount of debt used in buyout transactions. Their key findings are that "there appears to be no discernible relation between leverage in buyout firms and median leverage of public firms in the same industry-region-year... Cross-sectional characteristics such as industry fixed effects or variables such as profitability, earnings volatility, and growth opportunities, which explain most of the variation in public company leverage, have little explanatory power for buyout leverage. ... The one robust predictor of LBO leverage we find is the prevailing condition of debt markets: the higher the credit risk premium of leveraged loans, ... the lower the leverage used in buyout transactions." Using further tests, they find results on the cost of capital that support an agency story: higher leverage is associated with higher transaction prices and lower equity returns.

Haddad *et al.* (2017) investigate the timing of buyout deals. Their key finding is that "buyout activity decreases when the aggregate risk premium is high and increases when it is low. This factor alone explains over 30% of the total variation in buyout activity, more than three times the variation explained by credit market conditions." Intuitively, the gains to operational improvements are decreasing in the risk premium – long-term cash flows are more valuable when discount rates are lower. Since the cost of concentrated ownership is increasing in the risk premium, buyout funds that take concentrated positions to make operational improvements are doubly advantaged by lower risk premiums. The authors present supporting evidence in the cross-sectional and time-series patterns of buyout targets' systematic and idiosyncratic risks.

In related work, Martos-Vila *et al.* (2019) show that debt market (mis-)valuations strongly impact the relative presence of strategic and financial bidders, with more overvaluation ("cheap debt") associated with more financial bidders, i.e., buyout. In their model, overvaluation by outside investors favors financial buyers because they are buying the firm as a stand-alone operation (a sort of pure play), while strategic buyers combine the target with existing projects. For strategic buyers, overvalued debt reduces the perceived value of coinsurance across projects. In addition, overvaluation makes governance more valuable, and PE governance is thought to be better. They use the ex post accuracy of credit ratings to proxy for debt mis-valuation, and show that mis-valuation is strongly associated with financial, not strategic, bidders.

To the best of our knowledge, these sets of results have not been reconciled:

Open Question 24: What is the combined role of debt and equity pricing in the timing and financing composition of buyout deals?
It seems puzzling that the timing should be driven by the equity risk premium and financing composition should be driven by credit market conditions. However, this may be linked to the separation in

time between LP and GP decision making (see Open Question 22). Answering this question would be of wider interest because of its relevance to the overall M&A literature.

6.5.2   Theories of Buyout Financing and Activity

Models that explain the structure of PE funds and the complementarities in BO activities have emphasized the role of debt. Axelson *et al.* (2009) use an adverse selection investment model to explain fund structure: debt is deal-by-deal, but equity is pooled by the fund and fees are paid out of aggregate excess returns. Why is equity not split up like debt? Deal-by-deal debt prevents the GP from investing in bad deals in bad times, while pooled equity generates incentives to avoid bad deals in good times. The GP is then given a levered-equity residual which strongly resembles carried interest. This model also generates pro-cyclical investment with counter-cyclical performance, in that all projects, including bad ones, can more easily be funded in good times relative to bad times.

Malenko and Malenko (2015) argue that GPs borrow against assets and also against reputational capital. A large fraction of a GPs compensation for success takes the form of future fees from raising larger funds, and so a GP must be concerned with not just the ability to borrow today, but the ability to borrow in the future. Thus, GPs play a dynamic game and have a reputation. Since those same GPs are tempted by the standard debt/equity conflicts, the need for GPs to borrow in the future can make borrowing easier today. Value added through operational improvements and financing decisions are complements: higher levels of GP skill implies there will be more good deals in the future and raises the value of the future relative to the present. This in turn makes reputational capital more important and enables more borrowing today. More, low overall discount rates also make the future relatively more important, thus low discount rates lead to more borrowing through the reputational channel.

However, no model of which we are aware separates the role of investment timing from the role of financing composition and treats

LPs and GPs as constrained agents that operate with a time-varying equity risk premium:

> **Open Question 25: How well can a model that separately considers investment timing and financing composition explain buyout activity?**
> *This is the complement to the empirical Open Question 24, and it would be of interest to the wider M&A literature.*

6.6 Theories of Optimal Allocation and Liquidity Management

Next we consider theories of portfolio choice and liquidity management. Early management tools for estimating future exposures and cash flows include, for example, Takahashi and Alexander (2002). In this section, we focus on models with stochastic shocks.

To begin, we can observe that many of the frictions in PE have analogues in public equity markets, and the literature describing those frictions in the public equities context is well developed. The surveys of Vayanos and Wang (2012) and Vayanos and Wang (2013) create a taxonomy of liquidity effects in public markets, organizing the question of "what is liquidity?" That said, different liquidity frictions overlap and interact in the private equity context. The results, as we discuss below, do not resemble the sum of frictions in the public equity context.

In this section, we will first outline public equity liquidity frictions and their connection to private equity. Then, we move to explicitly private-equity-based theories and what they predict for LP investment.

6.6.1 Public Equity Theories of Liquidity and Their Relation to PE

The surveys of Vayanos and Wang (2012) and Vayanos and Wang (2013) group theories of liquidity into six different fundamental frictions: participation costs, transaction costs, asymmetric information, imperfect competition, funding constraints, and search. All of these would seem to apply, one way or another, in a private equity setting:

(1) Participation costs: It appears as though larger LPs have an advantage over smaller ones. First, minimum commitment sizes

are standard and funds of funds seem to perform relatively poorly, at least in BO (see, e.g., Section 6.1). Second, PE investments are opaque enough to require significant due diligence (see Section 5.2).

(2) Transaction costs: Transactions in the secondary market – attempts to sell LP stakes – occur at a discount (See Sections 2.3 and 6.3).

(3) Asymmetric information: Some LPs have skill, which generates an adverse selection problem for those without it. More, informational holdup is a plausible explanation for several stylized facts (see Sections 5.1 and 5.2).

(4) Imperfect competition: Both LPs and GPs appear to have some pricing power (see Sections 5.1 and 5.2).

(5) Funding constraints: LPs promise funding liquidity to the GP when they pledge capital to be called at a later date (See Section 2). In addition, LPs are likely have funding liquidity needs of their own. An endowment or pension fund, for example, would have relatively fixed obligations that needs to be met.

(6) Search: There is no centralized exchange on which LPs and GPs find each other. More, the persistence of LP–GP pairings over funds suggests that there may be some sort of lock-in effect (see Sections 5.1 and 5.2).

Asymmetric information and agency issues between LPs and GPs impact portfolio allocation decisions. One agency issue, the incentive for GPs to strategically manipulate valuations (especially for underperforming managers who need to raise a next fund), was already mentioned above. A second consideration is that not all LPs have access to all GPs, and access is at least in part determined by existing relationships, LP size, and GPs' expectations regarding funding stability from LPs (that is, the ability to honor capital calls in a timely manner). This means LPs do not all face the same opportunity set, and there are endogenous participation costs. Third, there is substantial heterogeneity in GP skill, and some LPs are skilled in assessing manager quality, generating adverse selection problems for unskilled LPs. However, the information asymmetry regarding LP skill also yields pricing power for LPs, which results in outperformance after fees, and performance persistence. This can also be a problem in models of over-the-counter trade, and there are parallels to the hedge fund environment, but the scale of the problem in PE is larger.

6.6.2 PE-Specific Liquidity Frictions

There are several additional features of private equity liquidity that do not have clear analogues in public markets.

First, investments by LPs and distributions to LPs are lumpy and the timing is uncertain. The timing is selected by the GP – by making a capital commitment that the GP can call when needed, the LP has written an option on their funds to the GP.[6] Put differently, LPs provide funding liquidity to the GP. Then, once capital is invested, selling LP stakes is expensive and time-consuming. Similarly, fund distributions are sporadic and endogenous. Empirically, net capital usage is counter-cyclical in the sense that net capital demands increase in bad times. Finally, after capital is returned, reinvestment opportunities vary, especially given that an LP's preferred GPs may not be raising new funds at the time of reinvestment. The costs of investing with a new GP are high (e.g., costs associated with vetting and due diligence).

Second, the LP can diversify across funds in ways that change their liquidity exposure. For example, diversifying across funds diversifies across capital call and distribution timing, leaving only systematic timing risk. But, this can result in overlapping pledges: spreading out investment timing can mean relying on older capital distributions to fund newer capital pledges. This funding mismatch can increase exposure to systematic shocks. In response, LPs may need to hold more liquid assets to meet capital calls when they occur. Then, after capital calls, portfolio weights change mechanically, and LPs may want to rebalance.

Third, there does exist a secondary market, so the LP can trade out of their position at a loss that is usually not too large. A fully liquid

---

[6]Lock-up periods in hedge funds bear a passing resemblance, but they are not quite equivalent in scale or implementation.

secondary market would alleviate the problems of counter-cyclical capital usage by allowing LPs to purchase liquidity when needed. In particular, an LP could use the sale of existing investments to fund commitments to new ones. However, the secondary market can dry up, and empirically, it has disappeared precisely when liquidity needs were greatest (e.g., during the 2008–09 financial crisis). In fact, Albuquerque *et al.* (2018), in a sample from a secondary market intermediary, shows that aggregate (market) liquidity is an important determinant of secondary market prices.

6.6.3   Theories of Allocation and Liquidity

There is a developing theoretical literature that evaluates LP investments.

An earlier liquidity literature studies deterministic lock-ups, meaning the duration of the lock-up is certain and known in advance (e.g., Longstaff, 2009). However, an LP's investments are locked up for an uncertain duration: the GP distributes funds when they exit their portfolio company investment, so we are particularly interested in stochastic restrictions on trade. Ang *et al.* (2014) look at stochastic market closures and compare them to different types of illiquidity in welfare and optimal portfolio allocation. The key finding is that trading illiquidity begets funding illiquidity: if the agent's portfolio tilts too far toward illiquid assets, intermediate consumption cannot be made smooth. Illiquidity has a large effect on welfare and premia only when the agent is prevented from optimally consuming for long periods of time, and stochastic market closures (e.g., failures of search) have the largest impact. More, the risk of entering a crisis (i.e., illiquidity risk, as opposed to illiquidity) creates premia and portfolio restrictions even during liquid times.

Sørensen *et al.* (2014) assume that investments are locked up for 10 years, there is no secondary market, and an appreciable fraction of private equity investment risk is unspanned by public markets. They find that the cost of illiquidity is large, and comparable in size to the value of the GPs' fees. If PE funds can borrow at the risk-free rate, the GP must earn an alpha of about 2% for the LP to break even in welfare terms. Dimmock *et al.* (2019) build on Sørensen *et al.* (2014) by adding a secondary market with proportional transaction costs and by allowing the PE asset to pay a dividend and have periodic purchases and liquidations. Investment alphas of 1% to 3% justify LP allocations of 13% to 60% to alternative investments. Bollen and Sensoy (2016) add more detailed spending rules for the LP, and therefore more detailed funding liquidity needs, as well as a secondary market. Calls and distributions have stochastic timing, and the timing of distributions is affected by fund performance. In a calibration using available PE returns, they find that large allocations to private equity can be sustained if secondary markets are very liquid. Otherwise, LPs need access to above average GPs to justify large allocations.

Giommetti and Sørensen (2021) present a model of private equity in which capital calls and distributions are smooth over time, appealing to the law of large numbers to reflect an investor who is diversified across funds but must choose how to allocate commitments over time. The key friction is that LPs must keep a liquidity reserve to fund their uncalled commitments. The paper's result is that, across a range of risk aversions and situations, LPs should keep 15%–25% of their total wealth invested in PE, with an additional 17%–24% of their wealth in uncalled capital commitments. Over time, high-risk-aversion LPs respond to positive shocks to their PE investment by scaling back commitments – they target an interior optimum. In contrast, low-risk-aversion LPs are restrained by the liquidity reserve and keep commitments high.

Gourier *et al.* (2021) present a model of PE that emphasizes the role of capital commitment; LPs commit to a discrete number of funds ($N = 1, 2, \infty$) and capital is called stochastically. This commitment risk has two parts: investors will have a stochastic waiting time, and during that time public markets will move, changing the fraction of wealth that is eventually called ("the denominator effect"). The welfare premium associated with uncertainty over the length of delay is almost zero, and may even be negative, while the premium associated with the relative quantity called is large. The investor can optimally diversify by mixing quantities across funds, but the welfare premium associated with commitment does not decrease much. The agent risks a funding mismatch, in which earlier funds pay out a little late, while later funds call a little early, and the investor is squeezed for liquid funds. This risk is exacerbated with private equity and liquidity cycles. Moreover, the public market denominator effect is common to commitments across funds so cannot be diversified away. Finally, different forms of liquidity appear to be complements because increased liquidity increases allocations, which in turn increases other liquidity premiums; for example, a more liquid secondary market increases the welfare premium associated with commitment risk.

The general takeaway from these papers is that illiquidity needs to be priced, and that current returns (alphas) are near what is required. That said, optimal portfolio policies appear to be relatively sensitive to measured alphas, justifying a wide range of portfolio policies for different institutions (with difference access or pricing power). However, the literature is limited, and there are some clear needs in order to understand an LP's allocation decision:

Open Question 26: How can models of LP liquidity management be generalized?

How should an LP manage their different liquidity needs? Given all the different types of illiquidity, which ones are qualitatively and quantitatively important in PE? PE investments have minimum commitment sizes, idiosyncratic and systematic liquidity shocks, and pay-in and pay-out timing are both correlated with changes in valuations, which are also systematic and idiosyncratic. How should an LP commit their funds so as to manage idiosyncratic liquidity events? More generally, what is the optimal way for LPs to structure commitments across different funds? Is this impacted by agency problems within an LP?

Gourier et al. (2021) and Giommetti and Sørensen (2021) make significant progress on this question from a portfolio choice perspective, but there is substantially more to do. Maurin et al. (2020) (described in 5.2) provide an explanation for LP liquidity diversification based on GP agency problems. How can these results be extended and generalized?

The models above are fundamentally portfolio choice problems from the perspective of a single LP. However, the PE equity industry has matured over time and realized LP returns have changed, both across time and across LP types (see Section 5.1). A natural consequence of participation costs is that this maturation should be associated with changes in the composition of LPs, and these compositional changes should in turn impact PE's returns:

Open Question 27: How have private equity holdings changed as a result of macroeconomic trends and cycles, and maturation of the PE industry?

The restrictions on LP investment imply that investors cannot move freely into private equity, and VC LPs may differ systematically from BO LPs. How much of aggregate private equity holdings are driven by changes in the composition of LPs, and how much are driven by changes in portfolio allocation for existing LPs? Has this changed as the industry has matured and secondary markets have become more liquid? Is there a persistent relationship across the PE liquidity cycle?

What is the theoretical linkage between individual LP participation and PE cycles? What do we expect the relative contribution of the intensive and extensive margins of participation to be?

7

Conclusion

We organize the literature on portfolio allocation to private equity around the perspective of the limited partner, including performance measurement and evaluation, the skills and pricing power of both LPs and GPs, and a discussion of liquidity and diversification. While much progress has been made in studying the private equity portfolio problem, our survey highlights how much remains to be explored. We include 27 open research questions and opportunities, which we hope will help guide future research towards a more complete model of asset allocation with private equity.

Acknowledgements

We are grateful to an anonymous referee, Ulf Axelson, Elise Gourier, Jarrad Harford, Lukas Kremens, Ludovic Phalippou, Morten Sørensen, Chester Spatt, Per Strömberg, and Sheridan Titman for comments and discussion.

List of Open Questions

References

Acharya, V. V., O. F. Gottschalg, M. Hahn, and C. Kehoe (2013). "Corporate governance and value creation: Evidence from private equity". *The Review of Financial Studies.* 26(2): 368–402.

Agrawal, A. and P. Tambe (2016). "Private equity and workers' career paths: The role of technological change". *The Review of Financial Studies.* 29(9): 2455–2489.

Albertus, J. F. and M. Denes (2020). "Private equity fund debt: Capital flows, performance, and agency costs". Unpublished working paper. Tepper School of Business.

Albuquerque, R., J. Cassel, L. Phalippou, and E. Schroth (2018). "Liquidity provision in the secondary market for private equity fund stakes". Unpublished working paper. Boston College, Carroll School of Management.

Aliaga-Díaz, R., G. Renzi-Ricci, H. Ahluwalia, D. M. Grim, and C. Tidmore (2020). "The role of private equity in strategic portfolios". *Vanguard Research.*

Andonov, A., Y. V. Hochberg, and J. D. Rauh (2018). "Political representation and governance: Evidence from the investment decisions of public pension funds". *The Journal of Finance.* 73(5): 2041–2086.

Andonov, A., R. Kräussl, and J. D. Rauh (2020). "The subsidy to infrastructure as an asset class". Unpublished working paper. University of Amsterdam.

Ang, A., B. Chen, W. N. Goetzmann, and L. Phalippou (2018). "Estimating private equity returns from limited partner cash flows". *The Journal of Finance*. 73(4): 1751–1783.

Ang, A., R. J. Hodrick, Y. Xing, and X. Zhang (2006). "The cross-section of volatility and expected returns". *The Journal of Finance*. 61(1): 259–299.

Ang, A., D. Papanikolaou, and M. M. Westerfield (2014). "Portfolio choice with illiquid assets". *Management Science*. 60(11): 2737–2761.

Anson, M. J. (2002). "Managed pricing and the rule of conservatism in private equity portfolios". *Journal of Private Equity*. 5: 18–30.

Anson, M. J. (2007). "Performance measurement in private equity: Another look". *Journal of Private Equity*. 10: 7–21.

Axelson, U., T. Jenkinson, P. Strömberg, and M. S. Weisbach (2013). "Borrow cheap, buy high? The determinants of leverage and pricing in buyouts". *The Journal of Finance*. 68(6): 2223–2267.

Axelson, U., M. Sörensen, and P. Strömberg (2014). "Alpha and beta of buyout deals: A jump CAPM for long-term illiquid investments". Unpublished working paper. LSE, Dartmouth, and Stockholm School of Economics.

Axelson, U., P. Strömberg, and M. S. Weisbach (2009). "Why are buyouts levered? The financial structure of private equity funds". *The Journal of Finance*. 64(4): 1549–1582.

Baker, M. and P. Gompers (2003). "The determinants of board structure at the initial public offering". *Journal of Law and Economics*. 46(2): 569–598.

Banal-Estañol, A., F. Ippolito, and S. Vicente (2017). "Default penalties in private equity partnerships". Unpublished working paper. Universitat Pompeu Fabra and Universidad Carlos III.

Barber, B. M., A. Morse, and A. Yasuda (2021). "Impact investing". *Journal of Financial Economics*. 139(1): 162–185.

Barber, B. M. and A. Yasuda (2017). "Interim fund performance and fundraising in private equity". *Journal of Financial Economics*. 124(1): 172–194.

Barberis, N. (2000). "Investing for the long run when returns are predictable". *Journal of Finance*. 55: 225–264.

Barberis, N. and M. Huang (2008). "Stocks as lotteries: The implications of probability weighting for security prices". *American Economic Review*. 98(5): 2066–2100.

Begenau, J. and E. Siriwardane (2020). "How do private equity fees vary across public pensions?" Unpublished working paper. Stanford Graduate School of Business.

Berk, J. B. and R. C. Green (2004). "Mutual fund flows and performance in rational markets". *Journal of Political Economy*. 112(6): 1269–1295.

Bernile, G., D. Cumming, and E. Lyandres (2007). "The size of venture capital and private equity fund portfolios". *Journal of Corporate Finance*. 13(4): 564–590.

Bernstein, S., X. Giroud, and R. R. Townsend (2016). "The impact of venture capital monitoring". *The Journal of Finance*. 71(4): 1591–1622.

Bernstein, S. and A. Sheen (2016). "The operational consequences of private equity buyouts: Evidence from the restaurant industry". *The Review of Financial Studies*. 29(9): 2387–2418.

Bharath, S., A. Dittmar, and J. Sivadasan (2014). "Do going-private transactions affect plant efficiency and investment?" *The Review of Financial Studies*. 27(7): 1929–1976.

Biesinger, M., Ç. Bircan, and A. Ljungqvist (2020). "Value creation in private equity". Unpublished working paper. Darmstadt University of Technology.

Black, F. and R. Litterman (1990). "Asset allocation: Combining investor views with market equilibrium". *Fixed Income Research, Goldman Sachs*.

Black, F. and R. Litterman (1992). "Global portfolio optimization". *Financial Analysts Journal*. 48(5): 28–43.

Bollen, N. P. B. and B. Sensoy (2016). "How much for a haircut? Illiquidity, secondary markets, and the value of private equity". Unpublished working paper. Vanderbilt University.

Boucly, Q., D. Sraer, and D. Thesmar (2011). "Growth LBOs". *Journal of Financial Economics*. 102(2): 432–453.

Boyer, B., T. D. Nadauld, K. P. Vorkink, and M. S. Weisbach (2018). "Private equity indices based on secondary market transactions". Unpublished working paper. Brigham Young University.

Brandt, M. W., A. Goyal, P. Santa-Clara, and J. R. Stroud (2005). "A simulation approach to dynamic portfolio choice with an application to learning about predictability". *Review of Financial Studies.* 18: 831–873.

Braun, R., T. Jenkinson, and C. Schemmerl (2020). "Adverse selection and the performance of private equity co-investments". *Journal of Financial Economics.* 136(1): 44–62.

Braun, R., T. Jenkinson, and I. Stoff (2017). "How persistent is private equity performance? Evidence from deal-level data". *Journal of Financial Economics.* 123(2): 273–291.

Brennan, M. J. (1998). "The role of learning in dynamic portfolio decisions". *Review of Finance.* 1: 295–306.

Brown, G. W., E. Ghysels, and O. Gredil (2020a). "Nowcasting net asset values: The case of private equity". Unpublished working paper. University of North Carolina and Tulane University.

Brown, G. W., O. R. Gredil, and S. N. Kaplan (2019). "Do private equity funds manipulate reported returns?" *Journal of Financial Economics.* 132(2): 267–297.

Brown, G., R. Harris, W. Hu, T. Jenkinson, S. N. Kaplan, and D. T. Robinson (2021). "Can investors time their exposure to private equity?" *Journal of Financial Economics.* 139(2): 561–577.

Brown, G., W. Hu, and B.-K. Kuhn (2020b). "Private investments in diversified portfolios". Unpublished working paper. University of North Carolina (UNC) at Chapel Hill.

Buchner, A. and R. Stucke (2014). "The systematic risk of private equity". Unpublished working paper. University of Passau and University of Oxford.

Campbell, J. Y. and R. J. Shiller (1988). "The dividend-price ratio and expectations of future dividends and discount factors". *Review of Financial Studies.* 1(3): 195–228.

Cavagnaro, D. R., B. A. Sensoy, Y. Wang, and M. S. Weisbach (2019). "Measuring institutional investors' skill at making private equity investments". *The Journal of Finance.* 74(6): 3089–3134.

Chakraborty, I. and M. Ewens (2018). "Managing performance signals through delay: Evidence from venture capital". *Management Science.* 64(6): 2875–2900.

Chen, P., G. T. Baierl, and P. D. Kaplan (2002). "Venture capital and its role in strategic asset allocation". *Journal of Portfolio Management.* 28: 83–89.

Chevalier, J. A. (1995). "Do LBO supermarkets charge more? An empirical analysis of the effects of LBOs on supermarket pricing". *The Journal of Finance.* 50(4): 1095–1112.

Choi, W., A. Metrick, and A. Yasuda (2013). "A model of private equity fund compensation". In: *Global Macro Economy and Finance.* Ed. by F. Allen, M. Aoki, N. Kiyotaki, R.Gordon, and J. Stiglitz. Vol. III. *International Economic Association, Proceedings of the Sixteenth World Congress.* Palgrave Macmillan. 271–286.

Chung, J.-W. (2012). "Performance persistence in private equity funds". *SSRN Electronic Journal.*

Chung, J.-W., B. A. Sensoy, L. Stern, and M. S. Weisbach (2012). "Pay for performance from future fund flows: The case of private equity". *The Review of Financial Studies.* 25(11): 3259–3304.

Cochrane, J. H. (2005). "The risk and return of venture capital". *Journal of Financial Economics.* 75(1): 3–52.

Cochrane, J. H. (2021). "Portfolios for long-term investors". Unpublished working paper. Stanford University.

Cohn, J. B., E. S. Hotchkiss, and E. M. Towery (2021a). "The motives for private equity buyouts of private firms: Evidence from U.S. corporate tax returns". Unpublished working paper. UT Austin, Boston College, and University of Georgia.

Cohn, J. B., L. F. Mills, and E. M. Towery (2014). "The evolution of capital structure and operating performance after leveraged buyouts: Evidence from U.S. corporate tax returns". *Journal of Financial Economics.* 111(2): 469–494.

Cohn, J. B., N. Nestoriak, and M. Wardlaw (2021b). "Private equity buyouts and workplace safety". *The Review of Financial Studies.* 34(10): 4832–4875.

Couts, S., A. S. Gonçalves, and A. Rossi (2020). "Unsmoothing returns of illiquid funds". Unpublished working paper. University of Southern California, University of North Carolina, and University of Arizona.

Da Rin, M. and L. Phalippou (2017). "The importance of size in private equity: Evidence from a survey of limited partners". *Journal of Financial Intermediation*. 31: 64–76.

Davis, S. J., J. Haltiwanger, K. Handley, R. Jarmin, J. Lerner, and J. Miranda (2014). "Private equity, jobs, and productivity". *American Economic Review*. 104(12): 3956–3990.

Degeorge, F., J. Martin, and L. Phalippou (2016). "On secondary buyouts". *Journal of Financial Economics*. 120(1): 124–145.

DeLuce, A. (2020). "Private equity fees and terms study". Callan Institute Research Study.

Demiroglu, C. and C. James (2012). "How important is having skin in the game? Originator-sponsor affiliation and losses on mortgage-backed securities". *The Review of Financial Studies*. 25(11): 3217–3258.

Dimmock, S. G., N. Wang, and J. Yang (2019). "The endowment model and modern portfolio theory". *Working Paper*. Columbia University.

Dimson, E. (1979). "Risk measurement when shares are subject to infrequent trading". *Journal of Financial Economics*. 7(2): 197–226.

Driessen, J., T.-C. Lin, and L. Phalippou (2012). "A new method to estimate risk and return of nontraded assets from cash flows: The case of private equity funds". *The Journal of Financial and Quantitative Analysis*. 47(3): 511–535.

Dyck, A. and L. Pomorski (2015). "Investor scale and performance in private equity investments". *Review of Finance*. 20(3): 1081–1106.

Eaton, C., S. T. Howell, and C. Yannelis (2020). "When investor incentives and consumer interests diverge: Private equity in higher education". *The Review of Financial Studies*. 33(9): 4024–4060.

Emery, K. M. (2003). "Private equity risk and reward: Assessing the stale pricing problem". *The Journal of Private Equity*. 6(2): 43–50.

Ewens, M., A. Gorbenko, and A. Korteweg (2022). "Venture capital contracts". *Journal of Financial Economics*. 143(1): 131–158.

Ewens, M., C. M. Jones, and M. Rhodes-Kropf (2013). "The price of diversifiable risk in venture capital and private equity". *The Review of Financial Studies.* 26(8): 1854–1889.

Ewens, M. and M. Marx (2018). "Founder replacement and startup performance". *The Review of Financial Studies.* 31(4): 1532–1565.

Fang, L., V. Ivashina, and J. Lerner (2015). "The disintermediation of financial markets: Direct investing in private equity". *Journal of Financial Economics.* 116(1): 160–178.

Fisher, J. D., D. M. Geltner, and R. B. Webb (1994). "Value indices of commercial real estate: A comparison of index construction methods". *The Journal of Real Estate Finance and Economics.* 9(2): 137–164.

Fracassi, C., A. Previtero, and A. W. Sheen (2020). "Barbarians at the store? Private equity, products, and consumers". Unpublished working paper. UT Austin, Indiana University, and University of Oregon.

Franzoni, F., E. Nowak, and L. Phalippou (2012). "Private equity performance and liquidity risk". *The Journal of Finance.* 67(6): 2341–2373.

Fulghieri, P. and M. Sevilir (2009). "Size and focus of a venture capitalist's portfolio". *The Review of Financial Studies.* 22(11): 4643–4680.

Gârleanu, N., L. Kogan, and S. Panageas (2012). "Displacement risk and asset returns". *Journal of Financial Economics.* 105(3): 491–510.

Gârleanu, N. and L. H. Pedersen (2018). "Efficiently inefficient markets for assets and asset management". *The Journal of Finance.* 73(4): 1663–1712.

Geczy, C., J. Jeffers, D. K. Musto, and A. M. Tucker (2021). "Contracts with (social) benefits: The implementation of impact investing". *Journal of Financial Economics.* 142(2): 697–718.

Geltner, D. M. (1991). "Smoothing in appraisal-based returns". *The Journal of Real Estate Finance and Economics.* 4(3): 327–345.

Geltner, D. M. (1993). "Estimating market values from appraised values without assuming an efficient market". *Journal of Real Estate Research.* 8(3): 325–346.

Geltner, D., B. D. MacGregor, and G. M. Schwann (2003). "Appraisal smoothing and price discovery in real estate markets". *Urban Studies.* 40(5–6): 1047–1064.

Getmansky, M., A. Lo, and I. Makarov (2004). "An econometric model of serial correlation and illiquidity in hedge fund returns". *Journal of Financial Economics.* 74(3): 529–609.

Giommetti, N. and M. Sørensen (2021). "Optimal allocation to private equity". Unpublished working paper. Copenhagen Business School.

Glode, V. and R. C. Green (2011). "Information spillovers and performance persistence for hedge funds". *Journal of Financial Economics.* 101: 1–17.

Goetzmann, W. N., E. Gourier, and L. Phalippou (2019). "How alternative are private markets?" Unpublished working paper. Yale School of Management.

Goetzmann, W., J. Ingersoll, M. Spiegel, and I. Welch (2007). "Portfolio performance manipulation and manipulation-proof performance measures". *The Review of Financial Studies.* 20(5): 1503–1546.

Gompers, P. A. (1996). "Grandstanding in the venture capital industry". *Journal of Financial Economics.* 42(1): 133–156.

Gompers, P. A., W. Gornall, S. N. Kaplan, and I. A. Strebulaev (2020). "How do venture capitalists make decisions?" *Journal of Financial Economics.* 135(1): 169–190.

Gompers, P. A. and J. Lerner (1997). "Risk and reward in private equity investments". *The Journal of Private Equity.* 1(2): 5–12.

Gompers, P., S. N. Kaplan, and V. Mukharlyamov (2016). "What do private equity firms say they do?" *Journal of Financial Economics.* 121(3): 449–476.

Gompers, P. and J. Lerner (2000). "Money chasing deals? The impact of fund inflows on private equity valuations". *Journal of Financial Economics.* 55(2): 281–325.

Gorbenko, A. S. and A. Malenko (2014). "Strategic and financial bidders in takeover auctions". *The Journal of Finance.* 69(6): 2513–2555.

Gornall, W. and I. A. Strebulaev (2020). "Squaring venture capital valuations with reality". *Journal of Financial Economics.* 135(1): 120–143.

Gourier, E., L. Phalippou, and M. M. Westerfield (2021). "Capital commitment". Unpublished working paper.

Gredil, O. R. (2022). "Do private equity managers have superior information on public markets?" *Journal of Financial and Quantitative Analysis*. 57(1): 321–358.

Gredil, O. R., Y. Liu, and B. Sensoy (2020a). "Diversifying private equity". Unpublished working paper. The Ohio State University.

Gredil, O., B. Griffiths, and R. Stucke (2014). "Benchmarking private equity the direct alpha method". Unpublished working paper. Tulane University.

Gredil, O., M. Sørensen, and W. Waller (2020b). "Evaluating private equity performance using stochastic discount factors". Unpublished working paper. Tulane University.

Groh, A. P. and O. Gottschalg (2011). "The effect of leverage on the cost of capital of US buyouts". *Journal of Banking and Finance*. 35: 2099–2110.

Grossman, S. J. and J. E. Stiglitz (1980). "On the impossibility of informationally efficient markets". *The American Economic Review*. 70(3): 393–408.

Guo, S., E. S. Hotchkiss, and W. Song (2011). "Do buyouts (still) create value?" *The Journal of Finance*. 66(2): 479–517.

Gupta, A. and S. Van Nieuwerburgh (2020). "Valuing private equity investments strip by strip". Unpublished working paper. New York University, Stern School of Business.

Gupta, A., S. T. Howell, C. Yannelis, and A. Gupta (2020). "Does private equity investment in healthcare benefit patients? Evidence from nursing homes". Unpublished working paper. University of Pennsylvania, NYU, and University of Chicago.

Haddad, V., E. Loualiche, and M. Plosser (2017). "Buyout activity: The impact of aggregate discount rates". *The Journal of Finance*. 72(1): 371–414.

Hansen, L. P. and R. J. Hodrick (1980). "Forward exchange rates as optimal predictors of future spot rates: An econometric analysis". *Journal of Political Economy*. 88(5): 829–853.

Harris, R. S., T. Jenkinson, and S. N. Kaplan (2014a). "Private equity performance: What do we know?" *The Journal of Finance.* 69(5): 1851–1882.

Harris, R. S., T. Jenkinson, S. N. Kaplan, and R. Stucke (2014b). "Has persistence persisted in private equity? Evidence from buyout and venture capital funds". Unpublished working paper. Darden School of Business.

Harris, R. S., T. Jenkinson, S. N. Kaplan, and R. Stucke (2018). "Financial intermediation in private equity: How well do funds of funds perform?" *Journal of Financial Economics.* 129(2): 287–305.

Harvey, C. R. and A. Siddique (2000). "Conditional skewness in asset pricing tests". *The Journal of Finance.* 55(3): 1263–1295.

Hellmann, T. (2002). "A theory of strategic venture investing". *Journal of Financial Economics.* 64(2): 285–314.

Hellmann, T., L. Lindsey, and M. Puri (2007). "Building relationships early: Banks in venture capital". *The Review of Financial Studies.* 21(2): 513–541.

Higson, C. and R. Stucke (2012). "The performance of private equity". Unpublished working paper. London Business School and University of Oxford.

Hochberg, Y. V., A. Ljungqvist, and A. Vissing-Jørgensen (2014). "Informational holdup and performance persistence in venture capital". *The Review of Financial Studies.* 27(1): 102–152.

Hochberg, Y. V. and J. D. Rauh (2012). "Local overweighting and underperformance: Evidence from limited partner private equity investments". *The Review of Financial Studies.* 26(2): 403–451.

Hüther, N. (2021). "Do private equity managers raise funds on (sur)real returns? Evidence from deal-level data". Unpublished working paper. Indiana University.

Hüther, N., D. T. Robinson, S. Sievers, and T. Hartmann-Wendels (2020). "Paying for performance in private equity: Evidence from venture capital partnerships". *Management Science.* 66(4): 1756–1782.

Hwang, M., J. M. Quigley, and S. E. Woodward (2005). "An index for venture capital, 1987–2003". *The B.E. Journal of Economic Analysis & Policy.* 4(1): 1–45.

Inderst, R., H. M. Mueller, and F. Münnich (2006). "Financing a portfolio of projects". *The Review of Financial Studies*. 20(4): 1289–1325.

Ivashina, V. and J. Lerner (2018). "Looking for alternatives: Pension investments around the world, 2008 to 2017". Unpublished working paper. Harvard University.

Janeway, W. H., R. Nanda, and M. Rhodes-Kropf (2021). "Venture capital booms and start-up financing". *Annual Review of Financial Economics*. 13: 111–127.

Jeffers, J., T. Lyu, and K. Posenau (2021). "The risk and return of impact investing funds". Unpublished working paper. University of Chicago.

Jegadeesh, N., R. Kräussl, and J. M. Pollet (2015). "Risk and expected returns of private equity investments: Evidence based on market prices". *The Review of Financial Studies*. 28: 3269–3302.

Jenkinson, T., W. R. Landsman, B. Rountree, and K. Soonawalla (2020). "Private equity net asset values and future cash flows". *The Accounting Review*. 95(1): 191–210.

Jenkinson, T., M. Sousa, and R. Stucke (2013). "How fair are the valuations of private equity funds?" Unpublished working paper. University of Oxford.

Jia, N. and D. Wang (2017). "Skin in the game: General partner capital commitment, investment behavior and venture capital fund performance". *Journal of Corporate Finance*. 47: 110–130.

Johannes, M., A. Korteweg, and N. Polson (2014). "Sequential learning, predictability, and optimal portfolio returns". *Journal of Finance*. 69: 611–644.

Kahle, K. M. and R. M. Stulz (2017). "Is the US public corporation in trouble?" *Journal of Economic Perspectives*. 31(3): 67–88.

Kanniainen, V. and C. Keuschnigg (2003). "The optimal portfolio of start-up firms in venture capital finance". *Journal of Corporate Finance*. 9(5): 521–534.

Kaplan, S. N. and A. Schoar (2005). "Private equity performance: Returns, persistence, and capital flows". *The Journal of Finance*. 60(4): 1791–1823.

Kaplan, S. N. and B. A. Sensoy (2015). "Private equity performance: A survey". *Annual Review of Financial Economics.* 7(1): 597–614.

Kogan, L., D. Papanikolaou, and N. Stoffman (2020). "Left behind: Creative destruction, inequality, and the stock market". *Journal of Political Economy.* 128(3): 855–906.

Korteweg, A. (2019). "Risk adjustment in private equity returns". *Annual Review of Financial Economics.* 11(1): 131–152.

Korteweg, A. (2022). "Risk and return in private equity". Unpublished working paper. University of Southern California.

Korteweg, A. and S. Nagel (2016). "Risk-adjusting the returns to venture capital". *The Journal of Finance.* 71(3): 1437–1470.

Korteweg, A. and M. Sørensen (2010). "Risk and return characteristics of venture capital-backed entrepreneurial companies". *The Review of Financial Studies.* 23(10): 3738–3772.

Korteweg, A. and M. Sørensen (2017). "Skill and luck in private equity performance". *Journal of Financial Economics.* 124(3): 535–562.

Kraus, A. and R. H. Litzenberger (1976). "Skewness preferences and the valuation of risk assets". *The Journal of Finance.* 31(4): 1085–1100.

Kroll, Y., H. Levy, and H. M. Markowitz (1984). "Mean-variance versus direct utility maximization". *Journal of Finance.* 39: 47–61.

Laux, C. (2001). "Limited-liability and incentive contracting with multiple projects". *The RAND Journal of Economics.* 32(3): 514–526.

Ledoit, O. and M. Wolf (2004). "Honey, I shrunk the sample covariance matrix". *Journal of Portfolio Management.* 31: 110–119.

Lee, A. (2015). "How LPs are driving private equity fundraising". *International Financial Law Review.*

Lerner, J., J. Mao, A. Schoar, and N. R. Zhang (2022). "Investing outside the box: Evidence from alternative vehicles in private equity". *Journal of Financial Economics.* 143(1): 359–380.

Lerner, J. and A. Schoar (2004). "The illiquidity puzzle: Theory and evidence from private equity". *Journal of Financial Economics.* 72(1): 3–40.

Lerner, J., A. Schoar, and W. Wongsunwai (2007). "Smart institutions, foolish choices: The limited partner performance puzzle". *The Journal of Finance.* 62(2): 731–764.

Lerner, J., M. Sorensen, and P. Stromberg (2011). "Private equity and long-run investment: The case of innovation". *The Journal of Finance.* 66(2): 445–477.

Leslie, P. and P. Oyer (2009). "Managerial incentives and value creation: Evidence from private equity". Unpublished working paper. Stanford University.

Levy, H. and H. M. Markowitz (1979). "Approximating expected utility by a function of mean and variance". *American Economic Review.* 69: 308–317.

Li, Y. (2014). "Reputation, volatility and performance persistence of private equity". Unpublished working paper. Federal Reserve Board.

Litvak, K. (2004). "Governance through exit: Default penalities and walkaway options in venture capital partnership agreements". *Willamette Law Review.* 40(4): 771–778.

Litvak, K. (2009). "Venture capital limited partnership agreements: Understanding compensation arrangements". *The University of Chicago Law Review.* 76(1): 161–218.

Long, A. M. and C. J. Nickels (1996). "A private investment benchmark". Unpublished working paper. Alignment Capital Group.

Longstaff, F. A. (2009). "Portfolio claustrophobia: Asset pricing in markets with illiquid assets". *American Economic Review.* 99: 1119–1144.

Lopez-de-Silanes, F., L. Phalippou, and O. Gottschalg (2015). "Giants at the gate: Investment returns and diseconomies of scale in private equity". *Journal of Financial and Quantitative Analysis.* 50(July): 377–411.

Ma, S. (2019). "The life cycle of corporate venture capital". *The Review of Financial Studies.* 33(1): 358–394.

Malenko, A. and N. Malenko (2015). "A theory of LBO activity based on repeated debt-equity conflicts". *Journal of Financial Economics.* 117(3): 607–627.

Markowitz, H. (1952). "Portfolio selection". *The Journal of Finance.* 7(1): 77–91.

Marquez, R., V. Nanda, and M. D. Yavuz (2015). "Private equity fund returns and performance persistence". *Review of Finance.* 19(5): 1783–1823.

Martos-Vila, M., M. Rhodes-Kropf, and J. Harford (2019). "Financial versus strategic buyers". *Journal of Financial and Quantitative Analysis*. 54(6): 2635–2661.

Mathews, R. D. (2006). "Strategic alliances, equity stakes, and entry deterrence". *Journal of Financial Economics*. 80(1): 35–79.

Maurin, V., D. Robinson, and P. Strömberg (2020). "A theory of liquidity in private equity". Unpublished working paper. Swedish House of Finance.

McCourt, M. (2018). "Estimating skill in private equity performance using market data". Unpublished working paper. University of Melbourne.

McKenzie, M. and W. Janeway (2008). "Venture capital fund performance and the IPO market". Unpublished working paper. University of Cambridge.

Metrick, A. and A. Yasuda (2010). "The economics of private equity funds". *The Review of Financial Studies*. 23(6): 2303–2341.

Nadauld, T. D., B. A. Sensoy, K. Vorkink, and M. S. Weisbach (2019). "The liquidity cost of private equity investments: Evidence from secondary market transactions". *Journal of Financial Economics*. 132(3): 158–181.

Nanda, R., S. Samila, and O. Sorenson (2020). "The persistent effect of initial success: Evidence from venture capital". *Journal of Financial Economics*. 137(1): 231–248.

Opp, C. C. (2019). "Venture capital and the macroeconomy". *The Review of Financial Studies*. 32(11): 4387–4446.

Pastor, L. and R. F. Stambaugh (2003). "Liquidity risk and expected stock returns". *Journal of Political Economy*. 111(3): 642–685.

Peng, L. (2001). "Building a venture capital index". Unpublished working paper. Pennsylvania State University.

Peters, R. H. (2018). "Volatility and venture capital". Unpublished working paper. Tulane University.

Phalippou, L. (2008). "The hazards of using IRR to measure performance: the case of private equity". Unpublished working paper. University of Oxford.

Phalippou, L. (2009). "Beware of venturing into private equity". *Journal of Economic Perspectives*. 23(1): 147–166.

Phalippou, L. (2010). "Venture capital funds: Flow-performance relationship and performance persistence". *Journal of Banking & Finance.* 34(3): 568–577.

Phalippou, L. (2013). "Yale's endowment returns: Case study in GIPS interpretation difficulties". *The Journal of Alternative Investments.* 15(4): 97–103.

Phalippou, L. (2014). "Performance of buyout funds revisited?" *Review of Finance.* 18(1): 189–218.

Phalippou, L. (2020). "An inconvenient fact: Private equity returns and the billionaire factory". *The Journal of Investing.* 30(1): 11–39.

Phalippou, L. and O. Gottschalg (2009). "The performance of private equity funds". *The Review of Financial Studies.* 22(4): 1747–1776.

Phalippou, L., C. Rauch, and M. Umber (2018). "Private equity portfolio company fees". *Journal of Financial Economics.* 129(3): 559–585.

Preqin (2016). "Preqin special report: Private capital fund terms".

ProPublica (2009). "Yale's financial wizard, David Swensen, says most endowments shouldn't try to be like yale". URL: https://www.prop ublica.org/article/yales-financial-wizard-david-swensen-says-mos t-endowments-shouldnt-try-to-b.

Rezaei, M. A. (2020). "Optimal design of limited partnership agreements". Unpublished working paper. University of California, Berkeley.

Ritter, J. R. and I. Welch (2002). "A review of IPO activity, pricing, and allocations". *Journal of Finance.* 57: 1795–1828.

Robinson, D. T. and B. A. Sensoy (2013). "Do private equity fund managers earn their fees? Compensation, ownership, and cash flow performance". *The Review of Financial Studies.* 26(11): 2760–2797.

Robinson, D. T. and B. A. Sensoy (2016). "Cyclicality, performance measurement, and cash flow liquidity in private equity". *Journal of Financial Economics.* 122(3): 521–543.

Sagi, J. S. (2021). "Asset-level risk and return in real estate investments". *The Review of Financial Studies.* 34(8): 3674–3694.

Schillinger, P., R. Braun, and J. Cornel (2019). "Distortion or cash flow management? Understanding credit facilities in private equity funds". Unpublished working paper. Technische Universität München and Blackrock.

Sensoy, B. A., Y. Wang, and M. S. Weisbach (2014). "Limited partner performance and the maturing of the private equity industry". *Journal of Financial Economics*. 112(3): 320–343.

Sharpe, W. F. (1981). "Decentralized investment management". *The Journal of Finance*. 36(2): 217–234.

Sørensen, M. (2007). "How smart is smart money? A two-sided matching model of venture capital". *The Journal of Finance*. 62(6): 2725–2762.

Sørensen, M. and R. Jagannathan (2015). "The public market equivalent and private equity performance". *Financial Analysts Journal*. 71(4): 43–50.

Sørensen, M., N. Wang, and J. Yang (2014). "Valuing private equity". *The Review of Financial Studies*. 27(7): 1977–2021.

Spaenjers, C. and E. Steiner (2020). "Do private equity investors create value? Evidence from the hotel industry". Unpublished working paper. HEC Paris and Penn State University.

Stafford, E. (2022). "Replicating private equity with value investing, homemade leverage, and hold-to-maturity accounting". *The Review of Financial Studies*. 35: 299–342.

Stambaugh, R. F. (1999). "Predictive regressions". *Journal of Financial Economics*. 54: 375–421.

Stein, C. (1956). "Inadmissibility of the usual estimator for the mean of a multivariate normal distribution". In: *Proceeding of the Third Berkeley Symposium on Mathematical Statistics and Probability*. Ed. by J. Neyman. Berkeley. 197–206.

Takahashi, D. and S. Alexander (2002). "Illiquid alternative asset fund modeling". *The Journal of Portfolio Management*. 28(2): 90–100.

Van Binsbergen, J. H., M. W. Brandt, and R. S. J. Koijen (2008). "Optimal decentralized investment management". *The Journal of Finance*. 63(4): 1849–1895.

Vayanos, D. and J. Wang (2012). "Theories of liquidity". *Foundations and Trends in Finance*. 6(4): 221–317.

Vayanos, D. and J. Wang (2013). "Market liquidity – Theory and empirical evidence". In: *Handbook of the Economics of Finance*. Ed. by G. M. Constantinides, M. Harris, and R. M. Stulz. Vol. 2. Elsevier. Chap. 19. 1289–1361.

Woodward, S. E. (2009). "Measuring risk for venture capital and private equity portfolios". Unpublished working paper. Sand Hill Econometrics.

Xia, Y. (2001). "Learning about predictability: The effect of parameter learning on dynamic asset allocation". *Journal of Finance*. 56: 205–246.

Lightning Source UK Ltd.
Milton Keynes UK
UKHW020632080822
406998UK00005B/603